Innovation Skills and Leadership in Brazil's Public Sector

TOWARDS A SENIOR CIVIL SERVICE SYSTEM

OECD

BETTER POLICIES FOR BETTER LIVES

This document, as well as any data and any map included herein, are without prejudice to the status of or sovereignty over any territory, to the delimitation of international frontiers and boundaries and to the name of any territory, city or area.

Please cite this publication as:

OECD (2019), *Innovation Skills and Leadership in Brazil's Public Sector: Towards a Senior Civil Service System*, OECD Public Governance Reviews, OECD Publishing, Paris, *https://doi.org/10.1787/ef660e75-en*.

ISBN 978-92-64-48961-5 (print)
ISBN 978-92-64-55876-2 (pdf)

OECD Public Governance Reviews
ISSN 2219-0406 (print)
ISSN 2219-0414 (online)

The statistical data for Israel are supplied by and under the responsibility of the relevant Israeli authorities. The use of such data by the OECD is without prejudice to the status of the Golan Heights, East Jerusalem and Israeli settlements in the West Bank under the terms of international law.

Photo credits: Cover © patrice6000/Shutterstock.com and blurAZ/Shutterstock.com

Corrigenda to OECD publications may be found on line at: *www.oecd.org/about/publishing/corrigenda.htm*.

© OECD 2019

Foreword

Governments need to innovate to better address ongoing and emergent policy challenges and provide effective public services. For this to happen, the public sector needs to have access to the right capabilities including leadership skills.

OECD countries are increasingly introducing specific senior civil service (SCS) systems that ensure leaders are capable of achieving results. This study establishes a new assessment framework for SCS systems, based on the 2019 OECD Recommendation on Public Service Leadership and Capability. The framework looks at three aspects as they relate to public sector innovation: a) the necessary leadership skills, b) the available supply of these skills through competency mapping and development, and c) the demand for these skills through appointment processes and accountability tools.

The study uses data collected through surveys and workshops to identify skills gaps that civil servants perceive in their leadership, and identifies a set of needed leadership competencies gathered in consultation with Brazilian civil servants. The study also identifies an imbalance in supply and demand, with most of the existing initiatives aimed at building supply. The study recommends actions to better co-ordinate these supply-side interventions and to develop demand-side interventions such as merit-based recruitment processes (which a recent presidential decree has now made possible).

This study was conducted in parallel with, and complements, the companion study The Innovation System of the Public Service of Brazil: An exploration of its past, present and future journey. Together, they are meant to help Brazil develop a stronger, more deliberate approach to leadership and innovation.

The study also contributes to a broader debate on public leadership competencies in public sector innovation, and the systems needed to appoint the most effective people and support them in achieving results.

Acknowledgements

This study was prepared by the OECD Directorate for Public Governance (GOV), under the leadership of its Director, Marcos Bonturi.

This report was drafted by Cristina Mendes and Kevin Richman under the supervision of, and with contributions from Daniel Gerson, lead of the Public Employment and Management project. Edwin Lau, head of the Public Expenditure and Budgeting division, provided strategic orientations. Valuable comments and input were provided by colleagues in the OECD Observatory for Public Sector Innovation (OPSI) Marco Daglio and Alex Roberts. OPSI former colleague Supriya Trivedi designed the leadership skills framework, and former colleague Matt Kerlogue designed the beta version of the innovation skills framework used in this report.

This study also benefited from the insights provided by two peer reviewers: Simon Claydon, UK Revenue and Customs, and Chair of the Public Employment and Management Working Party, and Roland Edwards, US Department of Homeland Security.

Draft versions of this report have been shared and discussed with members of the Public Employment and Management working party (PEM), the Public Governance Committee (PGC), and the OECD's Global Network of Schools of Government. The report benefits greatly from detailed input from the PEM, which provided data and many rich case studies that are highlighted throughout.

The study benefitted from the inputs, reflections and contributions of numerous Brazilian stakeholders, obtained through interviews, discussions, workshops and correspondence. This study would not have been possible without the commitment and support of the Escola nacional de administração pública (ENAP) and their open and committed staff and Presidency members. We are particularly thankful for the unique assistance in collecting data and information, organising the team's fact-finding missions and workshops in Brasilia and providing feedback throughout the development of the review. The team would like to thank in particular Francisco Gaetani, Aline Soares, Diogo Costa, Guilherme de Almeida, Paulo Marques, Fernando Filgueiras, Diana Coutinho, Regina Souza, Marizaura Camões, Pedro Vilela, Rafael Cedro, Luna Viana, João Guilherme Granja and Jeanne Lina.

The OECD also expresses its gratitude to the Ministry of Economy (Ministério da Economia), then Ministry of Planning, Development and Management (Ministério do Planejamento, Desenvolvimento e Gestão), for its cooperation and input, in particular Gleisson Rubin, Luis Felipe Monteiro, Wagner Lenhart, Joelson Velloso, Soraya Brandão, Tito Froes, Luanna Roncaratti and Rodrigo Machado Molina.

Special thanks to Elisabeth Huggard and Javier Gonzalez for their administrative support and to Liv Gaunt for editorial assistance.

Table of contents

Foreword   3

Acknowledgements   5

Executive Summary   11

1. Leadership for a more productive public service   13
   Public leadership – a priority in OECD countries   16
   Leadership can promote a more efficient and productive public sector   18
   Leadership can reduce corruption risks and help rebuild trust in the public sector   22
   Leadership can develop and steer an innovative workforce   24
   Towards a model of supply and demand of leadership skills for innovation   27
   References   29

2. Contextualising leadership challenges in Brazil's federal administration   31
   Leadership within a complex and rigid career system   32
   A flexible and fragmented leadership cadre   33
   Turnover of senior civil service positions   38
   Findings of the OECD survey on core skills areas for public sector innovation in Brazil   39
   Notes   46
   References   47

3. Key skills for innovative leaders in Brazil's federal administration   49
   Evolution of the public sector leader   50
   Public sector leadership competency models   51
   Innovative leadership competencies for Brazil's federal administration   54
   Notes   63
   References   64

4. Developing the supply of innovation leadership in Brazil's federal administration   65
   Skills and competencies in Brazil's federal administration: An overview   66
   From bespoke to systemic: Moving away from classroom training to creating a learning culture
   for innovation in the senior civil service   71
   Recommendations and roadmap   79
   Notes   82
   References   83

5. Strengthening demand for a skilled leadership in Brazil's federal administration   85
   Job profiles and recruiting for innovation in the senior civil service   87
   Recommendations and roadmap   94
   Notes   97
   References   98

Tables

Table 2.1. Survey on Innovation Skills: Organisational Readiness Assessment: List of skills and subskills areas   42
Table 4.1. Roadmap for supply-side recommendations   80
Table 5.1. Minimal criteria for specific DAS and FCPE positions   92
Table 5.2. Roadmap for demand-side recommendations   95

Figures

Figure 1.1. Extent of the use of separate human resources management practices for senior civil servants in central government, 2016 and 2018   15
Figure 1.2. OECD Recommendation of the Council on Public Service Leadership and Capability table   18
Figure 1.3. General government expenditures by economic transaction as a percentage of GDP, 2014   19
Figure 1.4. Confidence in national government in 2017 and change since 2007   22
Figure 1.5. Ability, motivation and opportunity framework   25
Figure 1.6. Core skills areas for public sector innovation   26
Figure 1.7. Framework for public sector leaders to drive innovation   28
Figure 2.1. Most common differences between the employment framework of senior managers and that of regular staff, 2016   35
Figure 2.2. Average length of senior managers' tenure in a particular position, 2016   38
Figure 2.3. Profile of respondents to the OECD survey   40
Figure 2.4. Perception of capabilities on innovation skills in the federal, state and municipal administrations   41
Figure 2.5. Mapping innovation skills in Brazil's federal administration   43
Figure 2.6. Innovation skills: Self-perception by hierarchical level   44
Figure 2.7. Focus of employee surveys in OECD countries, 2016   45
Figure 3.1. Existence of a competency framework that enables a classification of skills and competencies for senior managers (leadership competencies)   51
Figure 3.2. Estonia's leadership competency model   52
Figure 3.3. Chile's Senior Executive Service System profile   53
Figure 3.4. Managerial behaviours for innovation (extract)   54
Figure 3.5. National School of Public Administration's leadership competency model   55
Figure 3.6. Leadership for innovation, an initial model for Brazil's civil service   56
Figure 3.7. Australian Public Service values   59
Figure 3.8. UK Civil Service Leadership Statement   62
Figure 4.1. Do civil servants who want to improve their innovation skills have the opportunity to do so?   67
Figure 4.2. Vision of Public Sector Leadership in the Netherlands   72
Figure 5.1. Common elements of selection processes for senior managers in OECD countries   88
Figure 5.2. Identifying senior managers in OECD countries   89
Figure 5.3. Accountability for merit in political appointments in OECD countries   90

Boxes

Box 1.1. Skills, competencies and leadership styles – some definitions   16
Box 1.2. OECD Recommendation of the Council on Public Service Leadership and Capability   17
Box 1.3. Why does political patronage result in worse public managers?   19
Box 1.4. The link between leadership and employee engagement   20
Box 1.5. How merit can reduce corruption risks   23
Box 1.6. Alliance for better people management in the public sector   24
Box 1.7. Abilities, motivation and opportunities   25

Box 1.8. Purpose and process of this review 27
Box 2.1. The public policy and government management specialists "career" 32
Box 2.2. Senior leaders in Brazil – some definitions 34
Box 2.3. Senior civil service recruitment and selection in Chile: 37
Box 2.4. OECD survey on the core skills areas for public sector innovation 39
Box 3.1. Values-driven leadership and culture in the OECD's Recommendation of the Council on Public Service Leadership and Capability 58
Box 3.2. Using values to shape culture in Australia's public sector 59
Box 3.3. The difference between leadership and management 60
Box 4.1. The Sigepe Talent Bank in the Brazilian federal administration 68
Box 4.2. Free Agents and GC Talent Cloud – Canada 68
Box 4.3. Investing in skills for public sector innovation in Spain 70
Box 4.4. Learning culture in the OECD Recommendation of the Council on Public Service Leadership and Capability 71
Box 4.5. Dutch vision of public sector leadership 72
Box 4.6. Developing a learning culture through Ireland's Civil Service People Strategy 73
Box 4.7. Canada's Digital Executive Leadership Program 74
Box 4.8. ENAP – School of Government 75
Box 4.9. Public Innovation Chair: A new approach to public policies in France 77
Box 4.10. Vetor Brasil: Networking for public sector impact 79
Box 5.1. Recommendation of the Council on Public Service Leadership and Capability 86
Box 5.2. Leadership competency assessment 88
Box 5.3. Merit-based senior civil service recruitment in Chile and Peru 91

Executive Summary

The Government of Brazil is currently tackling a core leadership challenge: improving civil service capability, productivity and innovation. This, in turn, requires a reconsideration of the skills and competencies needed in the senior ranks of public administrations, as well as an analysis of the mechanisms that reinforce these skills and competencies, and an evaluation of the incentives to innovate.

In Brazil, appointment criteria are neither systematic nor comprehensive, and often not based on technical or managerial standards for management positions. This presents risks for public innovation and, more broadly, for the quality of public policies. Initial steps have been taken to address this issue. A 2019 presidential decree establishes some minimum criteria for these positions and enables selection through merit-based processes.

This study examines the role of public leaders in driving innovation in Brazil's federal government, based on the OECD's Recommendation on Public Service Leadership and Capability. It first looks at the skills leaders need to steer an innovative civil service that meets today's needs and prepares for those of the future. Leadership competencies are clear statements about the skills and behaviours that a government expects from its leadership cadre. The OECD has identified three distinct but interconnected groups of leadership competencies for innovation, based on findings from interviews and workshops held in Brazil. These are:

- business acumen: skills to align processes and resources with innovation priorities. These include coalition building, strategic awareness, financial management, change management, project and people management, and accountability.
- innovation skills: the OECD has identified six skills areas for public sector innovation that need to be understood by senior leaders: iteration, data literacy, citizen centricity, curiosity, storytelling, and insurgency.
- mindsets: these approaches include courage, empathy, continuous learning, a focus on results, digital skills, interpersonal awareness, inspiration and empowerment.

The three skills areas above must sit on a solid foundation of ethics and public service values, which guide decision making towards the public interest. These skills groups could help adapt existing and future competency frameworks to the context of innovation in the Brazilian public sector.

Identifying the necessary leadership skills is not enough to drive more innovation in the public service. Once the skills have been identified, OECD countries often introduce a systematic approach to ensure their supply (for example, through learning and development) and demand by those who appoint leaders and hold them accountable. This is usually done through the development of a senior civil service (SCS) system, which sets skills standards and processes to ensure appointees meet those standards.

In Brazil, there are piecemeal interventions across the federal government that primarily focus on the supply side of skills, providing development opportunities for current and future leaders. Several institutions in the Brazilian federal administration have developed their own leadership development programmes, and the Brazilian School of Public Administration (ENAP) has often served as a "hub" for many of the leadership programmes while also developing its own. Organisations such as ENAP or the Ministry of Economy are also mapping civil servants' skills through a databank to ensure that those looking for talent will be able to reach beyond their own networks to find it.

These organisations are also playing an important role in bridging the gap between the public sector and civil society, the private sector, and academia. Brazilian civil society organisations have been particularly active in the fields of public sector innovation and better governance, helping to promote public leadership and innovation in Brazil. Civil society stakeholders have been working with different levels of government to help them apply competency-based approaches to the recruitment and development of public managers.

However, developing the supply of such skills among potential SCS will not produce results if there is no demand for these skills. Strengthening demand requires engagement and buy-in at the highest political levels. It also requires addressing risk-averse incentive structures so that leaders feel empowered to use the innovation skills they have.

As Brazil is building the foundations for a more coherent and comprehensive approach to innovation, the study recommends that the federal administration also consider the leadership conditions to support its vision of an innovative state. The study provides a roadmap to further develop a senior civil service system by recommending short-, medium- and longer-term actions to:

- Create a collaborative and unified view of innovative leadership
- Ensure leadership training is responsive, effective, and available
- Develop merit-based hiring practices that assess innovation competencies for management positions
- Include innovation-oriented objectives in job profiles and performance assessments.

This study's assessments provide a global picture of the areas that can support a more innovative and skilled leadership cadre in the Brazilian federal administration. Investing in building a skilled senior civil service would improve innovation and help Brazil successfully support a more effective and accountable federal public service.

1. Leadership for a more productive public service

This chapter builds a case for innovation leadership in Brazil's federal public administration. It reviews literature on the link between leadership and public governance outcomes, showing how leadership influences public service effectiveness and efficiency, and public sector innovation, to improve public services and rebuild trust in public institutions. The chapter concludes with a presentation of a model of supply and demand for leadership competencies, which serves as an analytical framework for the rest of the report.

The statistical data for Israel are supplied by and under the responsibility of the relevant Israeli authorities. The use of such data by the OECD is without prejudice to the status of the Golan Heights, East Jerusalem and Israeli settlements in the West Bank under the terms of international law.

Public service leaders in modern democracies are facing challenges which are increasingly complex and interconnected. In Brazil, as in all OECD countries, improving public service capability, productivity and innovation is increasingly necessary to meet citizens' expectations and rebuild trust in government. This is a fundamental leadership challenge. In order to meet this challenge, Brazil's federal administration is seeking to identify the skills, competencies and leadership styles required of the senior civil service (SCS) in a fit-for-purpose, innovation-ready public service. This report provides insight into these skills and competencies, and explores options to develop mechanisms and incentives that can enhance and reinforce public leaders' abilities to lead innovation in their organisations.

Brazil is not alone in facing this challenge. Across the OECD, women and men in senior management positions are expected to work across organisational boundaries, sectors and jurisdictions to design and implement innovative initiatives to address ongoing and emergent policy challenges and improve the impact of public services. They must balance competing objectives, manage and transform vast public organisations, motivate and inspire their workforces, and be trusted partners to citizens and an ever-growing list of partners and stakeholders within the public sector and beyond. Public service leaders are also asked to respond diligently to support fast-moving political agendas and react to unpredictable events and changes in society in accordance with the needs and expectations of elected officials, citizens and stakeholders.

These challenges are made more acute in a context of increasingly fast-paced and disruptive change, driven in part by an increasingly digital society and economy, including the public sector itself. Citizens expect services provided by their public sectors to leverage the opportunities presented by digital technologies while safeguarding their privacy and well-being. Rising to this challenge requires public service leaders with the skills, mindsets and tools to continuously innovate in an increasingly digital government, economy and society.

These leadership challenges are compounded by the fact that in many areas, public services are hampered by employment systems, policies and practices that were designed for a past context. In response, governments across the OECD and beyond are prioritising reforms that focus on institutionalising responsive, agile and innovative senior leadership to reform the civil services they lead.

In most OECD countries, public sector leadership is supported through some kind of SCS system, which aims to ensure that the administrative leaders at the top of the organisational hierarchy are equipped with appropriate skills and are supported throughout their tenures through separate policies, in recognition of their pivotal role in public service performance. Figure 1.1 shows to which degree these systems are developed in OECD countries. In Brazil, no such system exists yet, although elements are beginning to emerge (see Chapter 2).

Figure 1.1. Extent of the use of separate human resources management practices for senior civil servants in central government, 2016 and 2018

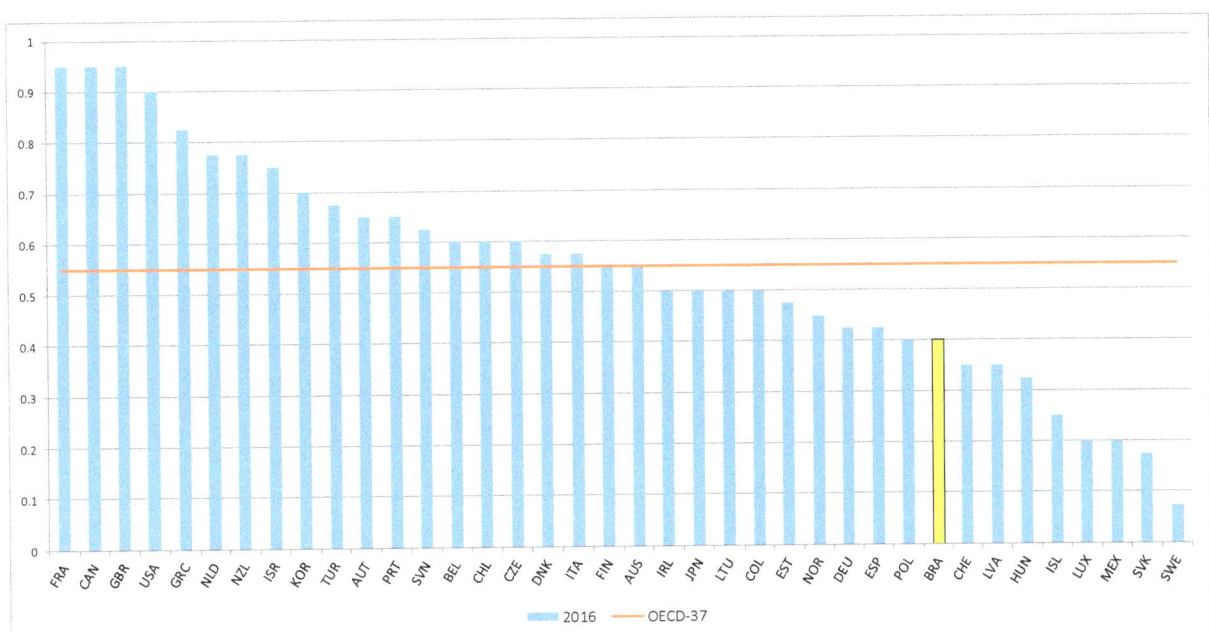

Notes: The index on senior civil service is composed of the following variables: the existence of a separate group of senior civil servants; the existence of policies for early identification of potential senior civil servants; the use of centrally defined skills profiles for senior civil servants; and the use of separate recruitment, performance management and performance-related pay practices for senior civil servants. The index ranges from 0 (no specific human resources management (HRM) practices for senior civil servants) and 1 (HRM practices very differentiated for senior civil servants). Missing data for countries were estimated by mean replacement. The index is not an indicator of how well senior civil servants are managed or how they perform. Slovak Republic: a new Civil Service Law entered into force on 1 June 2017, introducing major changes in existing human resources management practices. For this reason, data may no longer reflect the current situation in the country. Information on data for Israel: http://dx.doi.org/10.1787/888932315602.

Source: OECD (2016b), "Strategic Human Resources Management Survey". Data for Brazil prepared by the authors based on information collected during interviews, and refers to 2018.

This report provides recommendations for the development of an SCS system in Brazil, to ensure that the highest levels of the civil service are capable and supported to deal with the complex and interconnected societal problems of today and tomorrow. By way of introduction, this section makes the case for improving leadership in Brazil's federal public administration, arguing that better leadership contributes to a more efficient and productive public sector, improves services to citizens, and ultimately helps to rebuild trust in public institutions.

> ### Box 1.1. Skills, competencies and leadership styles – some definitions
>
> Despite broad use of the concept of "skill" in OECD, academic and governance literature, there is no universally agreed-upon definition. At its core, a skill is an ability to do something acquired through training and/or experience. Although most people probably have a sense of the word, there is a debate about how wide the definition should be. Should it include only measurable, observable skills, or also qualities related to behaviours and mindsets? This can have policy implications related to, for example, the ability to teach and develop some skills, versus behavioural traits which may appear harder to teach.
>
> Another challenge to the concept of skills is to define not only the what, but also the how. Moving from simple abilities (typing, reading) to the way these are combined to achieve impact in a job setting means moving from skills to competency. If writing is a skill, communication may be considered a competency.
>
> For the purposes of this report, the concept of competencies will be used to suggest the combination of skills with a focus on achieving desired results. Competencies often include behaviours (e.g. teamwork) and cognitive abilities (e.g. strategic thinking) that are less associated with individual skills. However, these terms are not very easy to distinguish and, in some cases, they may be used interchangeably.
>
> A third term, "leadership styles", is used to denote specific applications or groupings of leadership competencies. Leadership styles are the focus of various academic studies which look at, for example, transactional vs. transformation leadership, or adaptive leadership. These styles are further discussed in Chapter 3.

Public leadership – a priority in OECD countries

The context and challenges of the public service are changing at a fast pace, and the capabilities of public servants and those who lead them must constantly adjust. OECD countries increasingly recognise the fundamental contribution of effective public management and leadership to address complex governance challenges, and to enable public sector innovation. This is why OECD countries have worked together to develop the 2019 Recommendation of the Council on Public Service Leadership and Capability (hereafter referred to as the "Recommendation"; see Box 1.2).

The Recommendation sets out 14 principles that all OECD countries have agreed to work towards to ensure their public services are fit-for-purpose, responsive and capable of delivering quality service to society today and into the future. These principles are organised into three "pillars", which recommend that countries:

build a values-driven culture and leadership in the public service, centred on improving outcomes for society

invest in public service capability in order to develop an effective and trusted public service

develop public employment systems that foster a responsive and adaptive public service able to address ongoing and emerging challenges and changing circumstances.

The first pillar focuses on the role of public service leaders, and the need to "build a proactive and innovative public service that takes a long-term perspective in the design and implementation of policy and services". To achieve this, the OECD recommends governments take steps to provide senior civil servants with clear mandates and expectations regarding their role and behaviour, by:

clarifying the expectations incumbent upon senior-level public servants to be politically impartial leaders of public organisations, trusted to deliver on the priorities of the government, and uphold and embody the highest standards of integrity and

ensuring senior-level public servants have the mandate, competencies and conditions necessary to provide impartial evidence-informed advice and speak truth to power.

The OECD also recommends that countries find ways to advance these objectives by, "considering merit-based criteria and transparent procedures in the appointment of senior-level public servants, and holding them accountable for performance" and by "developing the leadership capabilities of current and potential senior-level public servants."

Box 1.2. OECD Recommendation of the Council on Public Service Leadership and Capability

Recommendations of the OECD Council make clear statements about the importance of an area and its contribution to core public objectives. They are based on agreed-upon principles of good practice and aspirational goals. The OECD's governing body, the Council, has the power to adopt Recommendations which are the result of the substantive work carried out in the OECD's committees. The end products include international norms and standards, best practices, and policy guidelines.

Recommendations are not legally binding, but practice accords them great moral force as representing the political will of member countries and there is an expectation that member countries will do their utmost to implement a Recommendation.

The Recommendation of the Council on Public Service Leadership and Capability is based on a set of commonly shared principles which have been developed in close consultation with OECD countries. This included a broad public consultation, which generated a high level of input from public servants, citizens and experts from around the world. This Recommendation joins a broad range of governance-related Recommendations on themes such as regulatory policy making, public sector integrity, budgetary governance, digital government strategies, public procurement, open government and gender equality in public life.

The Recommendation presents 14 principles for a fit-for-purpose the public service under three main pillars:

1. values-driven culture and leadership
2. skilled and effective public servants
3. responsive and adaptive public employment systems.

The full text of the Recommendation is available at: https://www.oecd.org/gov/pem/recommendation-on-public-service-leadership-and-capability-pt.pdf.

Figure 1.2. OECD Recommendation of the Council on Public Service Leadership and Capability table

1	2	3
Values-driven culture and leadership	Skilled and effective public servants	Responsive and adaptive employment systems
1. Defined values 2. Capable leadership 3. Inclusive and safe 4. Proactive and innovative	5. Right skills and competencies 6. Attractive employer 7. Merit-based 8. Learning culture 9. Performance- oriented	10. System stewardship 11. Strategic approach 12. Mobile and adaptive 13. Appropriate terms and conditions 14. Employee voice

OECD countries prioritise leadership in this Recommendation because they know from experience that it makes a difference. In all the efforts to implement better and more innovative governance, leadership is one of the fundamental enablers, or barriers, to successful change, whether related to improving public services, managing budgets more efficiently, improving transparency and accountability, or creating the conditions necessary for innovation in the public sector. As Brazil faces high fiscal pressure (see for example OECD 2018), effective leadership is a necessary ingredient of an efficient and productive public sector workforce. Leadership is also directly related to integrity and trust in public services. Finally, leadership is a necessary contribution to public service innovation. The next three sections look at these three areas in turn.

Leadership can promote a more efficient and productive public sector

Brazil invests significantly in its public sector workforce. In 2014, 11.9% of workers in Brazil were employed in the public sector, and the compensation of these public employees accounted for 28.9% of total government expenditures, and 12.9% of gross domestic product (GDP) (Figure 2.1). This investment in public workforce compensation is almost as much as the total level of expenditure in social benefits. An investment of this magnitude needs to be carefully managed to ensure its returns are maximised through policies and services that improve the lives and prosperity of its citizens. This is a call for innovative, skilled and professional public sector leadership.

Figure 1.3. General government expenditures by economic transaction as a percentage of GDP, 2014

Data for Brazil and selected Latin American and Caribbean countries

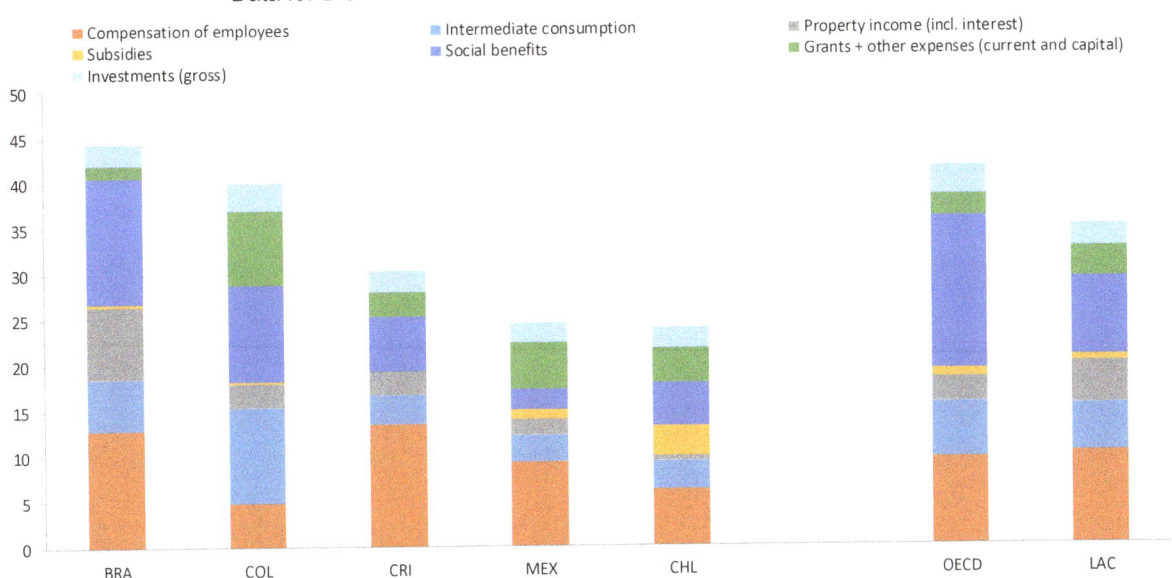

Note: LAC average includes Brazil, Chile, Colombia, Costa Rica, El Salvador, Mexico, Paraguay and Peru. Data for Costa Rica for investment do not include consumption of fixed capital. General government consists of central government, state government, local government and social security funds.
Source: IMF Government Finance Statistics (IMF GFS) database. Data for Mexico and the OECD average are based on the OECD National Accounts Statistics Database. Published in OECD (2016a), Government at a Glance Latin America and the Caribbean 2017, Chapter 2, http://dx.doi.org/10.1787/888933431042.

Research shows that the quality of leadership in the public sector impacts organisational performance, efficiency and productivity. Studies in the United States have shown that agencies led by career civil servants, rather than presidential appointees, tend to perform better (Gallo and Lewis, 2012). Furthermore, the quality of the presidential appointee matters. Appointees who were political operatives and campaign workers tended to perform worse than those from other areas (e.g. from academia or known policy experts) (Box 1.3). Similarly, a study on Chile and Peru suggests that public managers appointed through meritocratic mechanisms improve the spending of public funds and the internal management of public sector organisations (Cortázar, Fuenzalida and Lafuente, 2016). These findings are not surprising. The skills required by public managers and leaders are not the same as those required to run successful electoral campaigns, and meritocratic mechanisms assess those skills to attract and select the best possible candidate.

Box 1.3. Why does political patronage result in worse public managers?

Research summarised in Gallo and Lewis (2012) identifies two issues that may explain performance differences between leaders appointed from the political system and those from the career civil service in the context of the US system:

- Backgrounds and qualifications: appointees from outside the system generally have fewer years of public management experience, both within the agency they are appointed to lead and in the government overall. This creates greater information asymmetries between leaders and subordinates, which can make it challenging for leaders to monitor programmes' performance and implement new policy directions. Appointees, however, are likely to have closer political connections, more academic experience and/or more management experience from other sectors. However, Gallo and Lewis suggest that such experience is more difficult to leverage for improved organisational performance in the public sector, given the very different operating environments.

- Effects on the agency's personnel system: regardless of the appointees' actual skills and knowledge, they may display lower performance because they tend to have shorter tenures, which creates vacancies and higher turnover, which "makes it difficult for the agency to communicate agency goals, credibly commit to reform, monitor agency activity, and generally poorer performance". Furthermore, when appointees occupy top-level positions, career civil servants display less motivation and morale since these jobs appear out of their reach and are often filled by less qualified people.

Source: Gallo, N. and D.E. Lewis (2012), "The consequences of presidential patronage for federal agency performance", https://doi.org/10.1093/jopart/mur010.

Effective leaders can drive efficiency and productivity by creating the right conditions for employee engagement, a concept that is often measured and tracked through employee survey tools. Engaged employees are shown to perform better, and to be more productive and more innovative. They are committed to their organisation's mission and willing to go above and beyond their minimum job requirements to contribute to the success of their mission. Employee engagement is generally measured through employee surveys, and can thereby be linked empirically to improved organisational outcomes. In the private sector, studies show that firms with higher levels of employee engagement perform better on a range of indicators, including profit, productivity and innovation (see for example OECD 2016a).

The United Kingdom and the United States are leaders in the use of employee surveys to benchmark engagement across their public sector organisations. They show that one of the most important drivers of employee engagement is the quality of public sector leadership. Employee engagement therefore provides an important indicator of successful leadership and management (see for example OECD 2016b). Studies in the Canadian public service (see, for example, Treasury Board of Canada [2011]) have shown that more engaged employees provide a better service experience for citizens and thereby improve citizen trust in public services. Box 1.4 gives several examples.

Box 1.4. The link between leadership and employee engagement

Despite the differences in measuring employee engagement, studies conducted at the national level and based on employee surveys indicate that senior leadership is a key driver of employee engagement in the public service.

Australia: Based on the Australian Public Service employee census, effective leadership is a key contributor to employee engagement. When asked whether they thought senior leaders in their organisation were sufficiently visible, employees who strongly agreed showed substantially higher scores (double in some cases) on all components of employee engagement. Employees also value the opportunity to interact with their leaders in a meaningful way. In the Australian Public Service, leaders who engage their employees in how to deal with the challenges confronting their organisation have a very positive effect on the engagement levels of their employees (Australian Public Service Commission, 2013).

Canada: Employees who had positive opinions of senior management tended to express higher levels of engagement, particularly satisfaction with and commitment to their organisation. The most notable differences in levels of engagement are between employees who have confidence in senior management and those who do not (Treasury Board of Canada, 2011).

Ireland: Analysis based on the 2015 Civil Service Employee Engagement Survey revealed that the effectiveness of senior leadership was among the five key drivers of employee engagement along with employees' feeling that their job was meaningful, job skills match, competence and organisational support (Government of Ireland, 2016).

United Kingdom: Statistical analysis over several years of the UK People Survey scores consistently identifies leadership and effective change management as the strongest driver of employee engagement, followed by the nature of the work and an employee's relationship with their direct supervisor.

United States: The analysis of the 2016 Employee Viewpoint Survey revealed that important drivers of engagement were related to the ability of senior leaders to support fairness and protect employees from arbitrary actions, favoritism, political coercion and reprisal; promote and support collaborative communication and teamwork in accomplishing goals and objectives; and support an effective recognition and reward system for good performance.

Source: OECD (2016a), Engaging Public Employees for a High Performing Civil Service, http://dx.doi.org/10.1787/9789264267190-en.

Another way to think about the impact of public sector leadership is to look at success stories and, conversely, failures. The OECD's Observatory of Public Sector Innovation (OPSI) has collected hundreds of examples of successful public sector innovation projects that have improved the effectiveness and productivity of government. Of over 300 public sector innovation cases in the OPSI case study library, almost 80% cite leadership as a critical factor of success. This is equally true for innovations that come from the senior level (top-down) as it is for innovations that come from ideas at the frontlines (bottom-up) or from partners outside the public service. In all cases, committed and engaged senior leaders were needed to provide the support, protection and the linkages necessary to bring an idea to scale.

If good leadership can bring forward and stimulate successful innovation, the opposite is also true. All countries can think of public disasters which exposed leadership that was not well prepared for the task at hand. Various analyses of the US federal government's response to Hurricane Katrina have pointed to the head of the Federal Emergency Management Agency, who was appointed based on his political connections and was otherwise underqualified and inexperienced in the field of disaster management (see, for example, Schneider [2005]; Feeney and Kingsley [2008]). Many experts link Turkey's 2018 economic crisis, which saw the rapid devaluation of the currency, to the appointment of a central bank director with close family ties to the president (The Economist, 2019). Even in Canada, which has a very strong meritocratic leadership system, a recent auditor general's report suggested that a lack of effective leadership was in part to blame for the failure of a new pay system, which resulted in a web of complex pay problems that affected almost 200 000 federal civil servants (Office of the Auditor General of Canada, 2018).

These examples all illustrate the high stakes of appointment decisions in the public sector. These positions demand highly skilled and effective women and men who have the technical skills, leadership competencies and political awareness necessary to translate political ambition into effective policy and services. This is not a profile that can be developed on the campaign trail, or in the offices of political parties. When it goes well, it stands to transform countries' large investment in public sector workforces and the public services they provide into order and progress that ultimately leads to real development. When it goes poorly, it impacts not only the public workforce, but citizens and communities across the country, and contributes to societal issues and a crisis of trust in public institutions.

Leadership can reduce corruption risks and help rebuild trust in the public sector

As is the case in many other countries, Brazil is also struggling to rebuild trust in public institutions (Figure 1.4). Public leaders play a very important role in setting the ethical tone of an organisation and imparting the values that guide its decision making throughout. This means that leaders must themselves be ethical, and that they must also take active steps to encourage ethical behaviour in others.

Figure 1.4. Confidence in national government in 2017 and change since 2007

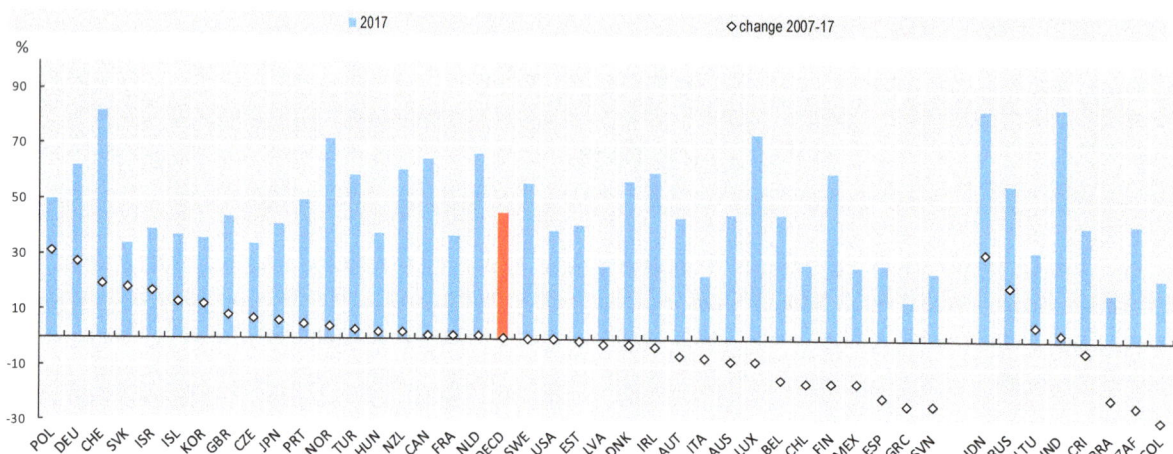

Note: Data refer to the percentage who answered "yes" to the question, "Do you have confidence in national government?" (data arranged in descending order according to percentage point change between 2007 and 2017). Austria, Croatia, Finland, Hungary, Ireland, Japan, Norway, Portugal, Slovak Republic, Slovenia and Switzerland: 2006 rather than 2007; Iceland and Luxembourg: 2008 rather than 2007.
Source: World Gallup Poll.

This is why the OECD's Recommendation of the Council on Public Service Leadership and Capability emphasises a values-driven culture and leadership in the public sector. Research on ethical leadership shows that values-based leadership requires two components (Treviño et al, 2000). The first is a leader who embodies the values of the public service, which are often separate from the specific political values of the elected government. Common public service values include integrity, accountability, protection of the public interest, openness and transparency. These values tend to be embraced in the culture of the public sector regardless of which political party is running the government.

The second component of values-based leadership is the ability to impart those values throughout the institution being led. This means openly discussing these values in an organisational context, supporting others to take decisions based on these values, and holding people accountable for values-based decision making at all levels of an organisation.

Promoting values-based leadership in the public service requires a careful look at the systems that are used to select and appoint leaders, and hold them accountable. Indeed, an important piece of recent research suggests that meritocratic appointment is the most important factor in reducing corruption risks in bureaucratic environments (Charron et al., 2017; see Box 1.2).

Ensuring merit in leadership selection means clearly articulating the leadership competencies needed to succeed in a job, then transparently matching candidates to those positions. It is possible to have merit and political appointments together – one does not necessarily preclude the other. However, it requires a level of transparency and some degree of contestability in the process in order to ensure accountability for those who take appointment decisions. This can be done through, for example, Senate confirmation hearings in the United States, or independent selection and vetting mechanisms such as those set up in Chile and Peru (see Chapter 5).

Box 1.5. How merit can reduce corruption risks

A merit-based senior civil service can help reduce overall corruption across all areas of the public sector. There are number of reasons for this. Charron et al. (2017) tested the hypothesis that corruption risks are lower when bureaucrats' careers do not depend on political connections but on their peers. The authors' findings suggest that:

1. Meritocratic systems bring in better-qualified professional leaders who may be less tempted by corruption.

2. Merit-based appointment creates an esprit de corps which rewards hard work and skills. When people are appointed for non-meritorious reasons, they may be less likely to see the position itself as legitimate, but instead as a means to achieve more personal wealth through rent-seeking behaviour. So there is also a motivational quality about merit systems which reinforces public service ethics and values.

3. Meritocracy has been shown to reduce the risk of corruption by providing longer term employment. This tends to promote a longer term perspective to decision making, which reinforces the employee's commitment to their job and makes it less tempting to engage in short-term opportunism presented by corruption. Conversely, if people know that their job will not last long, they may be more easily encouraged to use their position for personal gain during the short time they have.

4. The separation of careers between bureaucrats and politicians is also shown to provide incentives for each group to monitor one another and expose each other's conflicts of interest and risks for corruption. Conversely, when the bureaucracy is mostly political appointments, loyalty to the ruling party may provide disincentives for the bureaucracy to blow the whistle on political corruption (and elected officials may also be more willing to take action on corruption within the bureaucracy).

Source: Charron et al. (2017)

Merit-based selection also can have a direct impact on public trust in government institutions. If citizens believe that the public officials who are leading these institutions are there because they have the competencies and experience to make effective change happen, they may be more likely to trust them to deliver. On the other hand, if the public feels that these people are placed there for political reasons and lack the needed competencies and experience, it stands to reason that they will naturally trust them less.

The OECD has identified five drivers of trust in public services (OECD, 2017d). The first two are responsiveness and reliability, and these are related directly to the competence of public services. The other three are the underpinning values through which this competence is achieved. They are integrity, openness and fairness. The important implication here is that it is not enough to deliver effective public services in a democracy; the public's perception of the way they are delivered also counts. Achieving these three values in a visible manner is essential to rebuild trust in Brazil's public sector.

A clear starting point for rebuilding trust in Brazil's governance is the appointment of women and men who are seen by the Brazilian public to embody these two fundamental attributes. They must be seen as competent, demonstrated by having the right competencies and experience for the job. They must also show how public values guide their own decision-making, and be seen to impart these values throughout the entire organisation they lead.

Leadership can develop and steer an innovative workforce

Improving civil service capacity, productivity and innovation is a core leadership challenge. Innovation cannot be successful without support from public leaders with the right competencies. Effective leaders mobilise and engage staff to promote desired outcomes, and ensure that employees have the right resources and opportunities to use their skills and drive positive change in their organisations. Leaders also influence the strategy, structure and functioning of their organisations, as well as interactions with other public and private institutions.

Experience working with public sector innovators in Brazil and worldwide confirms that civil service leaders' commitment to innovation appears fundamental to support teams' and individuals' initiatives (OECD, 2017a). When there is a lack of leadership to drive change at the system or organisational level, individuals are left with the burden to drive change – limiting scope, scale and perspective. Initial impressions of the innovation system in Brazil's federal government suggest this to be the case (OECD, 2019). Research also suggests that capacity for innovation requires not only a system-wide approach and a co-ordinated effort across multiple institutions, but also greatly depends on building a skilled workforce and effective leadership (OECD, 2017c).

More than ever, Brazil's citizens and civil society are demanding better leadership from the top of the civil service. Organisations that usually advocate for better services in communities – such as education, healthcare and public safety – are increasingly concerned about the quality of leadership in public administrations, which they see as crucial for improving the quality of the essential services the public sector provides. They point to the need to spark more and better innovation in these services, and are worried that the public sector will no longer be able to attract the talent needed to do this. For this reason, they are taking direct aim at the process for hiring and the development of senior leadership, while trying to celebrate the positive impact that effective and innovative public leaders can bring.

Box 1.6. Alliance for better people management in the public sector

Improving the quality of people management in Brazil's public sector has attracted interest from beyond the public service itself. Brazilian foundations like Fundação Lemann are working to better understand the challenges faced by the public sector, and are helping governments to improve their human resources processes. Besides producing knowledge and organising events with public leaders, academics and the civil society, Fundação Lemann brought together three other Brazilian organisations (Instituto Humanize, Fundação Brava and Instituto República) to form an Alliance for better people management in the public sector.

The Alliance counts on its knowledge, experience and networks to help the public service attract and select better leaders. It supports State Governments across Brazil in fields as wide as preselection processes, leadership skills, performance management, skills development or knowledge transfer.

Source: Interviews, https://fundacaolemann.org.br

What would leadership for innovation look like in Brazil's public sector? A starting point is to recognise that public leaders create impact through their workforce. Then, it stands to reason that their first task is to ensure that their workforce is properly equipped to innovate and the organisation is properly oriented to produce innovation. People need three things to perform any task (Box 1.7). First, they need to right abilities: skills, competencies and knowledge. Second, they need to be motivated to develop these abilities and use them; this suggests looking at incentives and rewards. Third, they need opportunities to put their skills and motivation to use (Boxall and Purcell, 2011). Assuring these three elements for innovation is the fundamental leadership challenge in the public service.

Box 1.7. Abilities, motivation and opportunities

An established theory of employee behaviour states that civil servants and employees of any organisation will perform when they have the abilities, motivation and opportunities to contribute to their organisation's goals (Boxall and Purcell, 2011).

Figure 1.5. Ability, motivation and opportunity framework

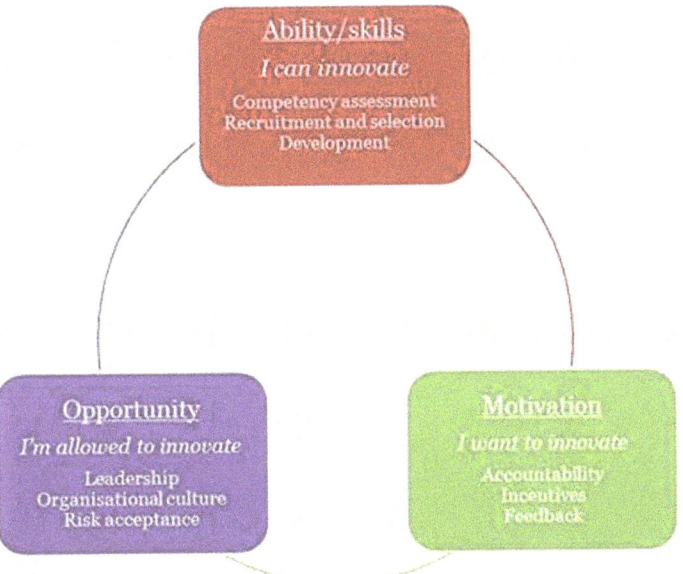

Source: Authors' own design

If innovation is the goal, then Brazil needs to develop and promote public sector leadership with the ability, motivation and opportunity to innovate. This framework reinforces the notion that having skills is not enough to drive performance if people are not motivated to use them, or provided the right opportunities to activate them. This means that teaching skills for innovation alone will not boost the innovative capacity of Brazil's public servants without taking a wider systems view of institutional structures (both supports and constraints) and workforce management. As such, this framework drives a systemic view, linking individual skills and capacities with the specific institutional features of the Brazilian public sector and its leadership, to increase and improve public sector innovation. This framework suggests that leaders should ask themselves:

1. **Abilities**: What are the needed skills for innovation in my organisation? Where can I find them? What are the gaps? What strategy can address them?

2. **Motivation**: What motivates my employees to innovate? How can I align incentives to promote the acquisition and use of innovation capabilities? How can I measure and monitor motivation in my workforce (e.g. through employee engagement surveys)?

3. **Opportunities**: How can I provide my employees with opportunities to innovate (e.g. safe spaces for experimentation)? How can I ensure they have access to the tools, resources and time needed? How can I create the right conditions in my organisation for innovation?

The OECD has developed research on the skills and competencies needed in public organisations at all levels of the hierarchy to support innovation. This research has identified six core skills areas (Figure 1.6). In order for public organisations to support innovation, their leadership should support and develop the following skills areas across their workforce as well as nurture a culture where these skills can thrive. Innovative organisations need employees who:

Know how to build new products, services or policies in iteration, beginning small, experimenting with ideas, and learning as they go.

Are able to leverage increasing amounts of data, in new shapes and forms, to spark insights and monitor progress.

Can use multiple methods and techniques to develop a deep understanding of the citizens they serve, their needs, wants and actual behaviours, and bring them into the design process.

Are curious, with the ability to ask the right questions of multiple sources, and find answers in new and novel places.

Have storytelling skills, to multiple audiences through various channels to ensure the change they want is understood and resonates with those it will impact, and those who must decide.

Have the skills needed to push against the status quo, to know how change is made in the public sector, by using the political process and building the right coalitions, knowing which battles to fight and persevere in the face of resistance. We call this insurgency.

Figure 1.6. Core skills areas for public sector innovation

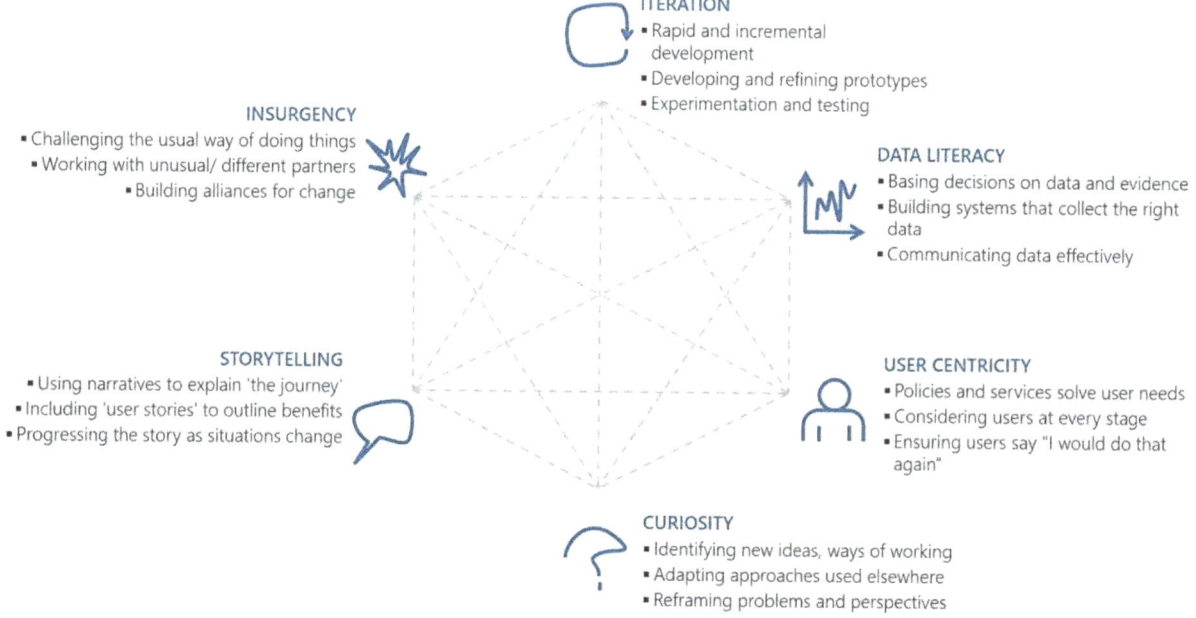

Source: OECD (2017a), "Core skills for public sector innovation: A beta model".

This report builds on this skills framework to pinpoint specific leadership skills, competencies and styles needed to drive innovation and impact in Brazil, and the systems in place to support and reinforce them (see Chapter 3 for a detailed discussion). The role of public leaders is not to be experts in all of these innovation skills areas. Rather, leaders must develop a workforce with these skills, motivate their use and provide employees with opportunities to contribute their skills to public sector innovation. This requires some understanding of each these skills areas and their implications on how to lead the workforce differently.

The survey presented in Chapter 2 shows that there are specific perceived gaps in Brazil's workforce in most of these skills areas. Results also suggest that access to training to develop these skills is either unknown or not available. These issues will be further discussed in the following chapters.

Towards a model of supply and demand of leadership skills for innovation

This report is the result of an analysis of some of the initiatives across the Brazilian administration. Based on research, observation, interviews and discussion (Box 1.8), this report aims to address the skills and leadership needs of Brazilian senior civil servants to promote innovation within their organisations and to achieve a more productive and accountable civil service.

Box 1.8. Purpose and process of this review

This is the first OECD review of this kind but it builds on previous work carried out by the OECD in this field, namely the 2010 Review of Human Resource Management in Brazil's Federal Administration (OECD, 2010), and the 2017 Review of Innovation Skills in Chile's Central Government (OECD, 2017b). The present review combined interviews and workshops with multiple Brazilian public sector and civil society stakeholders involved in civil service reform, leadership and innovation.

The first purpose of the discussions was to understand the institutional mechanisms that guide recruitment, development and performance assessment for senior civil servants in Brazil's federal government, in a context of increasing interest for capacity to innovate. Findings confirm those from previous studies that describe a fragmented civil service, with impacts on its performance. The second purpose was to map initiatives to strengthen different aspects of leadership capabilities, within a system where improving recruitment, development and assessment of senior managers tends to be voluntary organisational endeavour. The process included:

1. A survey with open questions (based on a theoretical framework on the abilities, motivations and opportunities of civil servants to innovate), was completed by the Brazilian National School of Public Administration (Escola nacional de administração pública, ENAP) and other stakeholders. The purpose was to collect initial data and evidence that would give the OECD team a broad and basic understanding of the civil service, public leadership and government innovation in Brazil's federal administration.

2. A first mission (May 2018) was made to get a contextual overview and deeper insights of the innovation and leadership landscape in Brazil's federal administration. This included interviews and focus group discussions with key public employees, senior leaders, academics and members of civil society. The OECD team was joined by a senior expert from the UK government with experience in civil service strategy and leadership development.

3. A second mission (September 2018) was made to conduct a series of workshops with Brazilian civil servants, members of civil society organisations and of academia. The workshops were designed around leadership skills for innovation and human resources sub-systems that support the identification, recruitment, development and performance assessment of innovative leaders. The workshops helped identify different scenarios that could work in Brazil's federal administration. In addition to the peer from the United Kingdom, this mission also included a representative from the United States' Chief Human Capital Officers Council. Both of these experts helped frame the discussions about leadership competencies and provided insights from practice.

4. A third mission took place during the 4th Innovation Week in Brasilia. It helped test some hypothesis about skills for innovative leaders and improving senior civil service management.

The report is guided by a framework established as a result of workshops and discussions with a range of public sector innovators, leaders, people managers, academics and civil society leaders, which led to the following insights. First, it is necessary to identify the leadership competencies and styles needed in the public service in order to support innovation in the public sector. However, identifying these competencies alone will not have much consequence unless they are integrated into a system that enables their development and effective deployment. This suggests the need for mechanisms to build the supply of these competencies in the possible pool of candidates through, for example, leadership development initiatives, and to make this supply visible in order to identify where these competencies are currently located. However, this will also not be enough, as supply without demand cannot lead to sustainable change. Therefore, the system must also build the demand for these competencies so that those with the responsibility of taking appointment decisions clearly request the desired competencies and create the right incentives for their use once appointed. This suggests looking at appointment systems and the incentive structures needed to make innovation a fundamental part of leaders' jobs.

Figure 1.7. Framework for public sector leaders to drive innovation

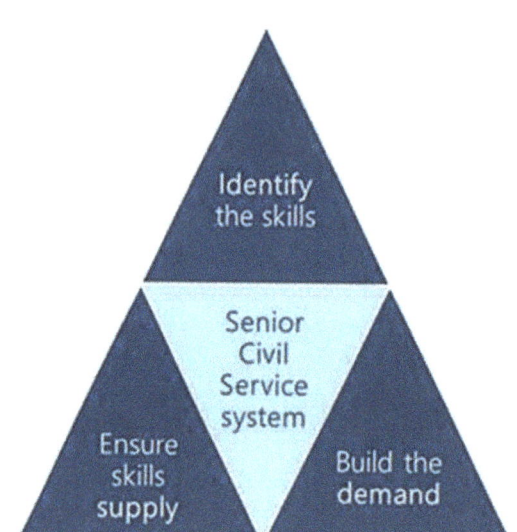

Source: Author's own design

his report will consider each element of this framework in turn, beginning with a contextualisation of the leadership challenges in Brazil's federal administration, followed by a discussion of the critical leadership competencies and styles as highlighted by Brazilian innovators and civil servants. It will then look at how the supply of, and demand for, the competencies in senior leaders can be reinforced through measures that could begin putting in place a more effective, coherent and sustainable SCS system.

Chapter 2 looks at the current state of public service leadership from a systems perspective, and with specific reference to innovation skills, presenting the results of a survey conducted by the OECD in December 2018 on the six innovation skills areas presented in Figure 1.4. This is followed by a discussion of the type of skills, mindsets and behaviours that leaders need to support innovation (Chapter 3). Chapter 4 analyses different initiatives that are aimed at developing current and future public leaders with these competencies within the federal administration. Chapter 5 suggests paths to build the demand for a skilled SCS cadre within a fragmented federal administration such as Brazil's.

References

Australian Public Service Commission (2013), "Employee engagement", Chapter 4 in: State of the Service Report: State of the Service Series 2011-12, Commonwealth of Australia, Canberra, https://www.apsc.gov.au/04-employee-engagement.

Boxall, P. and J. Purcell (2011), Strategy and Human Resource Management, Third Edition, Palgrave Macmillan.

Casa Civil (1994), Decreto n°1.171, de 22 de Junho de 1994 que Aprova o Código de Ética Profissional do Servidor Público Civil do Poder Executivo Federal, www.planalto.gov.br/ccivil_03/decreto/d1171.htm.

Charron, N. et al. (2017), "Careers, connections, and corruption risks: Investigating the impact of bureaucratic meritocracy on public procurement processes", The Journal of Politics, Vol. 79/1, pp. 89-104, https://doi.org/10.1086/687209.

Cortázar, J.C., J. Fuenzalida and M. Lafuente (2016), "Merit-based selection of public managers: Better public sector performance?: An exploratory study", IDB Technical Note, No. 1054, https://publications.iadb.org/en/merit-based-selection-public-managers-better-public-sector-performance-exploratory-study.

Feeney, M.K. and G. Kingsley (2008) "The rebirth of patronage: Have we come full circle?", Public Integrity, Vol. 10/2, pp. 165-176, http://dx.doi.org/10.2753/PIN1099-9922100205.

Gallo, N. and D.E. Lewis (2012), "The consequences of presidential patronage for federal agency performance", Journal of Public Administration Research and Theory, Vol. 22/2, pp. 219-243, https://doi.org/10.1093/jopart/mur010.

Government of Ireland (2016), Civil Service: Employee Engagement Survey 2015, prepared by the Department of Public Expenditure and Reform.

OECD (2019), The Innovation System of the Public Service of Brazil: An exploration of its past, present and future journey, OECD Publishing, Paris.

OECD (2018), Economic Survey of Brazil, https://www.oecd.org/eco/surveys/Brazil-2018-OECD-economic-survey-overview.pdf

OECD (2017a), "Core skills for public sector innovation: A beta model", OECD, Paris.

OECD (2017b), Innovation Skills in the Public Sector: Building Capabilities in Chile, OECD Public Governance Reviews, OECD Publishing, Paris, http://dx.doi.org/10.1787/9789264273283-en.

OECD (2017c), Skills for a High Performing Civil Service, OECD Public Governance Reviews, OECD Publishing, Paris, http://dx.doi.org/10.1787/9789264280724-en.

OECD (2017d), Trust and Public Policy: How Better Governance Can Help Rebuild Public Trust, OECD Public Governance Reviews, OECD Publishing, Paris, https://doi.org/10.1787/9789264268920-en.

OECD (2016a), Engaging Public Employees for a High Performing Civil Service, OECD Publishing, Paris, http://dx.doi.org/10.1787/9789264267190-en.

OECD (2016b), "Strategic Human Resources Management Survey", OECD, Paris.

Office of the Auditor General of Canada (2018), Reports of the Auditor General of Canada to the Parliament of Canada: Message from the Auditor General of Canada, Office of the Auditor General of Canada, http://publications.gc.ca/collections/collection_2018/bvg-oag/FA1-27-2018-1-0-eng.pdf.

Schneider, S.K. (2005), "Administrative breakdowns in the governmental response to Hurricane Katrina: Special report", Public Administration Review, Vol. 65/5, pp. 515-516, https://onlinelibrary.wiley.com/doi/pdf/10.1111/j.1540-6210.2005.00478.x.

The Economist (2019), "In the eye of the storm. Turkey is still on the brink of a recession", 3 January, The Economist, https://www.economist.com/europe/2019/01/05/turkey-is-still-on-the-brink-of-a-recession (accessed 4 April 2019).

Treasury Board of Canada (2011), "The People Management Excellence Drivers Model", https://www.tbs-sct.gc.ca/reports-rapports/pmt-gpt/2011-2012/pmt-gpt03-eng.asp

Treviño, L.K., L.P. Hartman and M. Brown (2000), "Moral person and moral manager: How executives develop a reputation for ethical leadership", California Management Review, Vol. 42/4, pp. 128-142, http://dx.doi.org/10.2307/41166057.

2. Contextualising leadership challenges in Brazil's federal administration

This chapter assesses current leadership challenges in Brazil's public service from a structural perspective, looking at the organisation of the workforce and the public service leadership. While Brazil's federal public service has strong merit-based entry, the career system presents particular rigidities which make it difficult to lead innovation in the public sector. In contrast, the high levels of flexibility among management positions present few opportunities to consider innovation competencies in leadership appointments. This chapter also looks at the results of a recent survey conducted for this review, which aims to assess the current state of specific innovation skills and competencies in the broader workforce.

Chapter 1 built a case for how leadership improves public sector outcomes for Brazil; in particular how it stands to develop a more productive, effective and accountable public service, and improve trust in the public sector. It calls for not only appointing qualified leaders, but also implementing a system that identifies needed leadership competencies, and builds both the supply and demand for these competencies.

This chapter assesses current leadership challenges in Brazil's public service from a systemic perspective, looking at the structures that organise the workforce and the public service leadership. It also looks at the results of a recent survey conducted for this review, which aimed to assess the current state of specific innovation skills and competencies.

Leadership within a complex and rigid career system

Brazil's federal career system presents particular challenges. The largest part of the workforce is grouped into around 300 "careers" (carreira). While some careers are similar to those of most countries (such as a diplomatic career), most careers appear to be equivalent to job categories. Often careers are attached to individual institutions with their own salary scales, although interministerial job categories have also been created, such as the specialist in public policy and government management career (EPPGG; see Box 2.1) (OECD, 2010).

Box 2.1. The public policy and government management specialists "career"

The career of specialist in public policy and government management (EPPGG) was designed for high-level public policy and management functions, along the lines of the French National School of Administration (Ecole nationale d'administration, ENA). The EPPGG was intended to facilitate the interface between the political and administrative levels of government. As such, EPPGG civil servants are expected to operate in all ministries and federal agencies, and facilitate public policy formulation and strategic management. To fulfil these expectations, EPPGG civil servants go through a common induction and initial training and can be assigned to positions throughout the administration. While in theory the EPPGG civil servants have greater opportunities for mobility than other careers, in practice mobility is not widespread. According to the Secretary of Management, 55% of EPPGG civil servants have stayed in the same area their entire career.[1]

The EPPGG has a government-wide role and is a corporate resource responsible for:

1. Public policy formulation: The EPPGG facilitates and supports public policy formulation by ensuring that decision makers receive well-formulated policy proposals and advice in all sectors of government.

2. Public policy implementation: The EPPGG supports decision makers by ensuring policies are implemented efficiently and effectively, and are accurately monitored and evaluated.

3. Government efficiency: The EPPGG develops and implements policies and programmes to improve the organisation and functioning of the government machine at macro and individual institution level.

In 2018, 44% of EPPGG civil servants had been appointed to senior management positions[2]. This is slightly more than other careers from the "management cycle", such as planning and budget analysts (analistas de planejamento e orçamento), finance and control analysts (analistas de finanças e controle) and foreign trade analysts (analistas de comércio exterior).

EPPGG civil servants work in a wide range of ministries, but are mainly concentrated in the then Ministry of Planning (27%), the Ministry of Justice and the Presidency (10% each).

Notes: 1. Secretary of Management, based on data from the Integrated System for Staff Administration (Sistema Integrado de Administração de Pessoal, SIAPE). 2. Senior Direction and Counselling Group (Grupo Direção e Assessoramento Superiores, DAS), "commissioned functions" (funções comissionadas do poder executivo, FCPE) or other positions that do not require participating in a competitive process (Secretary of Management, 2018)
Source: Secretary of Management (2018), Integrated System for Staff Administration.

Careers often have their own pay-setting process and salary structure, their own unions and staff associations. As such, when one career secures improvements to its salary or working conditions, this often leads to competition from others. This has led to a very fragmented workforce rather than one that can be strategically and collectively managed.

Against this backdrop, vertical career progression is often reduced to automatic seniority-based pay increments and lateral mobility is limited. The lack of a general classification system means that it is not possible to determine equivalent positions across ministries. Perhaps more importantly, the 1988 Constitution does not allow a public servant to move from one career to another without passing a new competitive examination. Successful civil servants enter at the starting point of the salary scale for the new job category, regardless of their former position and seniority.

In this context, leaders will likely have to manage teams from multiple careers, each with their own employment framework and own goals and objectives. This can make the development of horizontal skills, such as innovation skills, more challenging. It can also present challenges to the development of horizontal, multi-disciplinary teams that often create opportunities to innovate. Furthermore, once civil servants have accessed a career, there is very little strategic career development as promotions are based on seniority or appointment rather than performance or talent assessment. This has implications for both the development of skills and the motivation for their use.

A flexible and fragmented leadership cadre

Brazil's fragmented and rigid career system makes it challenging to identify who are the public leaders in its federal administration. Most OECD countries have some kind of senior civil service system, which serves to support and manage the most senior administrative leaders through separate merit-oriented policies in recognition of their pivotal role in public service performance. While Brazil's Constitution (Article 37) acknowledges specificities of some functions within the civil service (directors, managers and advisors), the people who perform these functions are not managed in the same way.

The DAS is Brazil's dominant system of senior managers. It is structured into six levels of management (operational, tactical and strategic management), DAS-6 being the highest ranking. Like in OECD countries, the higher the position, the lower the share of women (OECD, 2017b; Cavalcante and Lotta, 2015).

Additionally, a number of senior management positions are handled outside the DAS system, including senior positions through the FCPE. Until 2019, FCPE positions ranged from 1 to 4, with 4 being the most senior-ranked position. A law from June 2019[1] established that Level 5 and 6 FCPE positions may be created to replace same-level positions of DAS. The important difference between DAS and FCPE positions is that FCPE positions are reserved for civil servants, while anybody can be appointed to DAS positions.

For clarity and to ensure some degree of coherence with previous work, this report uses the same definition of senior leaders as the National School of Public Administration's 2018 staff report (ENAP, 2018) (Box 2.2). "Senior leaders" will thus refer to the highest levels of DAS (4, 5 and 6) and the FCPE (4).

Box 2.2. Senior leaders in Brazil – some definitions

Defining public sector leadership in Brazil, with its relatively fragmented public service, is a key challenge. The dominant system of senior managers – the Senior Direction and Counselling Group (DAS) includes non-managerial positions (see, for example, Cavalcante and Carvalho [2017]) and as such should not be considered a career, in particular from a managerial perspective (Pinheiro, 2017). Another important category of senior managers are the "commissioned functions" (FCPE). There are about 22 000 DAS and FCPE positions in the federal government (data from March 2018).

With these challenges in mind, the definition of "senior leadership" used in this report corresponds to the highest levels of DAS (4, 5 and 6) and FCPE (4). This classification is used by the Informe do Pessoal (staff report) of the National School of Public Administration (ENAP, 2018) and corresponds to the "cargos de alta direção" (senior management positions). These positions (especially DAS 5 and 6) have a relevant influence on the decision-making process and on the implementation of public policies. These 4 categories of DAS and FCPE comprise about 5 000 people in the executive (federal level of government).

Decree No. 5.497-2005 (modified by Decree No. 9.021-2017) established that 50% of DAS 4 positions should be reserved for career civil servants. Although the transformation of DAS into FCPE positions in 2016 also introduced new criteria for appointment (being a civil servant), it did not change the real nature of appointments. The same decree set a minimum limit of 60% of DAS 5 and 6 to be filled by public servants, which increased the number of public servants in those positions.

Law 13.844/2019 opened the possibility to transform DAS 5 and 6 into a new category of FCPE 5-6. This means that a larger number of positions would be reserved for career civil servants.

Sources: Cavalcante, P. and P. Carvalho (2017), "Profissionalização da burocracia federal brasileira (1995-2014): Avanços e dilemas", http://dx.doi.org/10.1590/0034-7612144002; Freire, A., P. Cavalcante and P. Palotti (2017), "Perfil e determinantes da ocupação de cargos comissionados no setor de infraestrutura do governo federal no Brasil"; ENAP (2018), Informe de Pessoal: Março 2018; Lopez, F. and S. Praça (2018), "Cargos de confiança e políticas públicas no executivo federal"; www.planalto.gov.br/ccivil_03/_Ato2004-2006/2005/Decreto/D5497.htm; www.planalto.gov.br/ccivil_03/_Ato2015-2018/2017/Decreto/D9021.htm.

The main difference between the management of the senior civil servants and the other civil servants relates mostly to the recruitment process, as the senior civil servants tend to be appointed rather than selected through a competitive examination. In addition, pay levels tend to be higher for the SCS, and assignments shorter, with turnover linked to the presidential mandate. The tenure of DAS 1-5 tends to be around 3.5-4 years (Cavalcante and Lotta, 2015). Despite these differences, there is no specific emphasis in the recruitment of the SCS, nor in the management of their careers, their performance or for avoiding conflicts of interest.[2]

Figure 2.1. Most common differences between the employment framework of senior managers and that of regular staff, 2016

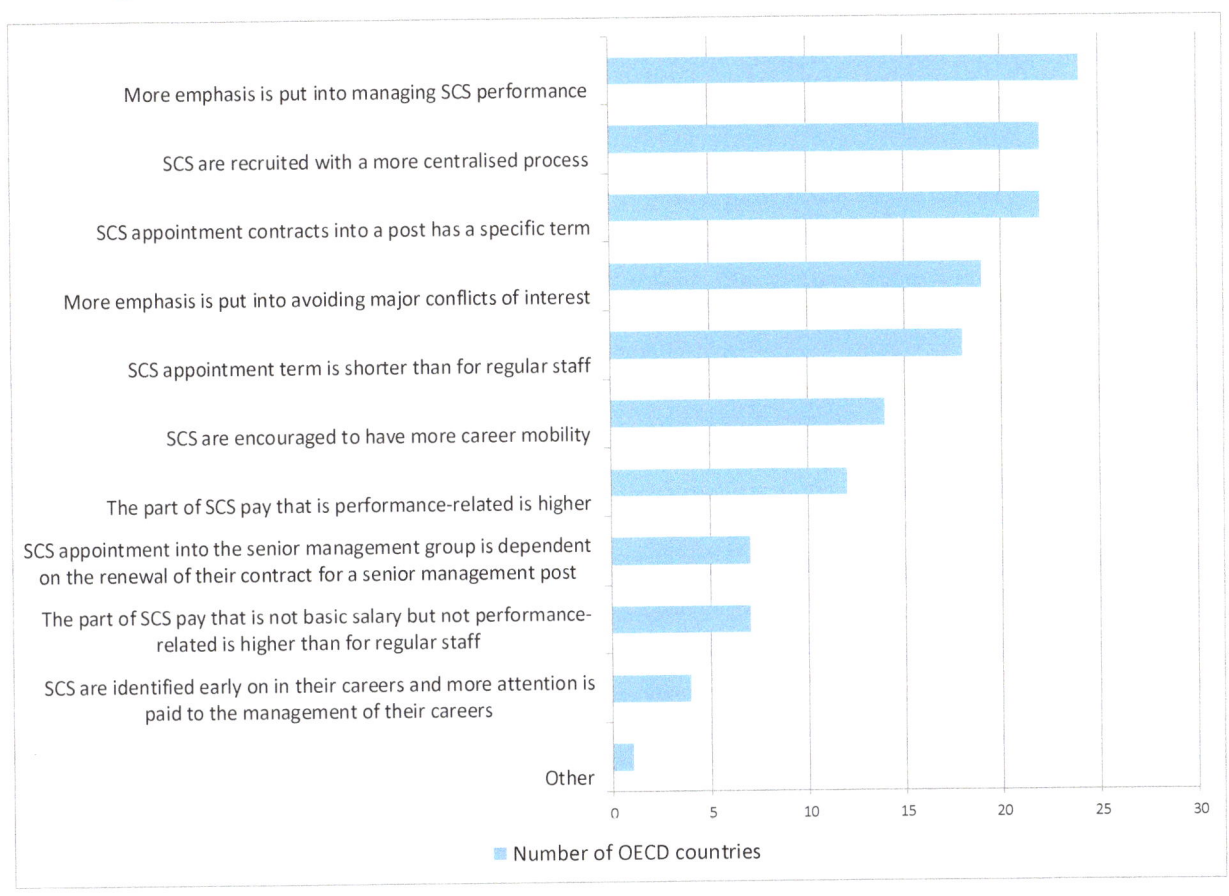

Note: SCS: senior civil servants. Response of 36 OECD countries to Question 85: "How different is the employment framework of senior managers from that of regular staff? [Q85] Please check all that apply".
Source: OECD (2016), "Strategic Human Resources Management Survey",
https://qdd.oecd.org/subject.aspx?Subject=GOV_SHRM

In the absence of an SCS system, appointments into DAS and FCPE leadership positions are, by definition, made at the will of the government and relevant hiring authorities. The management of DAS/FCPE appointments is usually delegated to each organisation (ministries and organisations directly subordinated to a ministry), which tend to have their own rules or procedures for the appointment process and responsibilities (OECD, 2010). While the centre of government (Casa Civil) approves appointments for the most senior DAS positions (Levels 4-6), there is no indication of a regular formal processes for examining senior management appointments (with the exception of investigation on compliance with integrity rules) (OECD, 2010).

The OECD's 2010 Review of Human Resource Management in Brazil's public sector found that "In Brazil, the main limitation of the SCS system is its lack of coherence and transparency in appointments" (OECD, 2010). The leadership appointment system could help bring a diversity of perspectives into the civil service, and provide career opportunities for public servants, regardless of their job category (OECD, 2010), helping to round out skills gaps and spark innovation (Pinheiro, 2017). However, in practice, appointment criteria are neither systematic nor comprehensive, and are often not based on technical or managerial standards for management positions (Cavalcante and Carvalho, 2017). Appointments to a vast number of managerial positions are independent of passing a competitive examination[3] and at the complete discretion of those who have the power to appoint. There seems to be no documentation of the reasons for specific DAS appointments, and no data are therefore available on why it was felt necessary or appropriate to select an external or internal candidate for a specific DAS appointment (OECD, 2010).

There is great heterogeneity in procedures, application forms and criteria, depending on the hiring and selection authority (Camões and Balué, 2015). In most cases there are no publicly available descriptions of requirements for SCS positions to be filled or of the merits of the persons selected, although some exceptions can be found in a reduced number of ministries (Pinheiro, 2017). At the same time, merit is still too strongly associated with academic and professional background (Camoes and Balué, 2015). As such, appointments to SCS positions usually do not tend to take into account predefined skill sets or behaviours in ways that assess candidates' abilities to address the complex challenges facing the country.

In Brazil, any significant change to the appointment criteria or definitions for SCS positions has to be approved by a normative act.[4] The focus of legal initiatives to improve the qualification of DAS/FCPE has been on ensuring that a significant number of senior-level appointees would come from the ranks of the civil service, including Decree No. 5.497-2005 and the creation of FCPE positions in 2016. While reserving a number of positions previously designated as DAS for civil servants may be a first step towards developing a structured career path in some management positions, these positions still fail to ensure any minimal level of senior management qualification and do not ensure any merit process in those political appointments. Indeed, being a civil servant is not, in and of itself, a "quality stamp" to become a senior manager (see, for example, Pinheiro [2017]; Lopez and Praça [2018]; Instituto República [2018]):

First, although civil servants went through selection processes at the beginning of their careers, the skills needed for entry-level positions are not the same as those needed for a leadership position. Despite being very selective, public competitions usually test theoretical knowledge.

Second, the training system for civil servants does not ensure that training is aligned with the skills and mindsets necessary to innovate and lead in today's public service. Up to 2019, the right to training for the SCS was regulated in a government decree of 2006[5], and civil servants had the right to a minimum number of hours of training every few years. This decree created the Policy for Civil Servant Development (Política Nacional de Desenvolvimento de Pessoal), which aimed, among others, to promote the managerial capacity building for civil servants, in order to help them qualify for DAS positions. By law, such training should be a priority in the training plans of the federal public administration.[6] ENAP promotes, elaborates and implements training for these positions; however, since there are no job descriptions nor clear performance objectives, the impact evaluation of the training remains limited and difficult to assess. A 2019 decree[7] establishes a people development plan (Plano de Desenvolvimento de Pessoas) and introduces new provisions about access to training (namely long-term training). Its implementation is due to start after the publication of this report[8] and as such is not included in the analysis.

Third, career progression within the civil service is automatic to a certain extent and disconnected from actual performance. It is automatic after a three-year probation period, because it is only based on the length of service and civil servants cannot be dismissed. In practice, it is possible to reach the top of a career after only ten years. The lack of an efficient performance assessment system implies that it is difficult to assess someone's performance throughout their career; and the SCS is simply not subject to individual performance assessments. When they do exist, evaluation systems do not tend to be aligned with the possibility to improve one's performance (Odelius, 2010) or the organisation's performance. At the same time, in cases of low performance[9], civil servants are directed to training or can benefit from an analysis of functional suitability.[10] Defining performance indicators could help clarify the SCS' contribution towards strategic organisational objectives, strengthen incentives to improve performance and identify potential skills gaps (OECD, 2017b). In the Brazilian context, the most common obstacles to implementing performance assessment systems appear to be resistance to evaluations, use of inadequate criteria, unclear results and unsuccessful integration of the performance system with other HRM systems (Odelius, 2010).

For these reasons, developing transparent job profiles and minimum qualifications for DAS and FCPE positions, independent of someone's status as a "civil servant", would be an opportunity to articulate the skills demanded for these positions. Decree No. 9.727-2019 is a first step to establish minimum criteria, profiles and procedures to recruit for DAS and FCPE positions and will be further discussed in Chapter 5. It indicates, for example, that recruiting administrations should have an updated job description for the highest SCS positions (DAS 5 and 6). This can help to better define expectations and ensure that high-level DAS and FCPE leaders have the means to lead their workforces to achieve innovative results.

At the same time, this is just a starting point, since the criteria outlined in the decree for these positions are rather broad. Furthermore, selection processes remain voluntary and the hiring authority has full discretion to appoint anyone that fulfils these criteria. The hiring minister may also appoint candidates who do not fulfil these criteria as long as s/he justifies the reasons behind the decision (for example the specificity of the position or the limited number of applications). While this may increase accountability for political appointments to a degree, this decree alone will not go very far in promoting the skills and conditions necessary innovative leadership in the federal administration.

Political appointments exist in most SCS systems and can be associated with a welcome degree of flexibility, in particular when they bring in highly qualified people from outside the public system (see, for example, OECD [2010]; Pinheiro [2017]). However, to achieve these benefits, OECD governments generally implement mechanisms to encourage appointments of people who have the experience and skills required for the job. Chile is one of the most commended examples with the introduction of a senior civil servant cadre (Sistema de Alta Dirección Pública).

Box 2.3. Senior civil service recruitment and selection in Chile:

Sistema de Alta Dirección Pública

In 2003, the Chilean government, with the agreement of all political actors (opposition political parties, non-governmental organisations, civil society), created the Sistema de Alta Dirección Pública (SADP), a central senior civil service system. The aim of the SADP was to establish a professional senior management. Following the reform, there are three distinct groups:

1. The most senior positions, which are filled by direct designation by the government (1 000 positions out of 2 million in central government).

2. The SADP, for which recruitment is based on public competition (1 000 positions in central government). There are two levels within the ADP: approximately 1% at the first hierarchical level (heads of service, directors general), and the remainder at the second hierarchical level (regional directors, heads of division).

3. Middle management positions (2 000 positions in central government) at the third hierarchical level, which form part of the career civil service.

The SADP has been implemented gradually by recruiting by open competition whenever a post falls vacant and by expanding it over time to additional groups. For example, it has been expended to include 3 600 municipal education directors and 2 800 new senior management posts in municipalities. Most of the selection process for the SADP is contracted out to specialised recruitment agencies.

The National Civil Service Directorate is responsible for management of the SADP. However, the Senior Public Management Council (Consejo de Alta Dirección Pública) is in charge of guaranteeing the transparency, confidentiality and absence of discrimination of the selection process. It is chaired by the director of the National Civil Service Directorate and has four members proposed by the president of Chile and approved by the Senate. The selection process, which takes about four months, begins with the publication of the vacancy in the media. A specialised enterprise commissioned by the Senior Public

Management Council analyses the curricula vitae of the different candidates and prepares a shortlist for the council or a selection committee (under the council's supervision).

Professional competence, integrity and probity are some of the criteria used in the selection process. Subsequently, the council or the committee selects the best candidates for interview and prepares a final shortlist for the competent authority for the final appointment.

The SADP was based on international experience. In particular, the experience of OECD countries such as Australia and New Zealand strongly influenced the Chilean model. The system is considered one of the main achievements of the modernisation of Chile's public management. One outcome has been the decline in the number of political appointees in the central government; they currently represent only 0.5% of the total public workforce. It is also argued that the presence of women in senior positions has increased under the system; they occupy 32% of positions, compared to 15% in the Chilean private sector.

Source: Weber, A. (2012), "Alta dirección pública".

Turnover of senior civil service positions

Turnover appears high[11] among SCS positions, likely a subsequent effect of the high turnover at the political level. While it was not possible to obtain data, experts estimated that many senior civil servants held their posts for around two to four years. In comparison, in most OECD countries senior managers stay at least three years in their position[12]; only Mexico reported that senior managers stay in their positions less than two years.

Figure 2.2. Average length of senior managers' tenure in a particular position, 2016

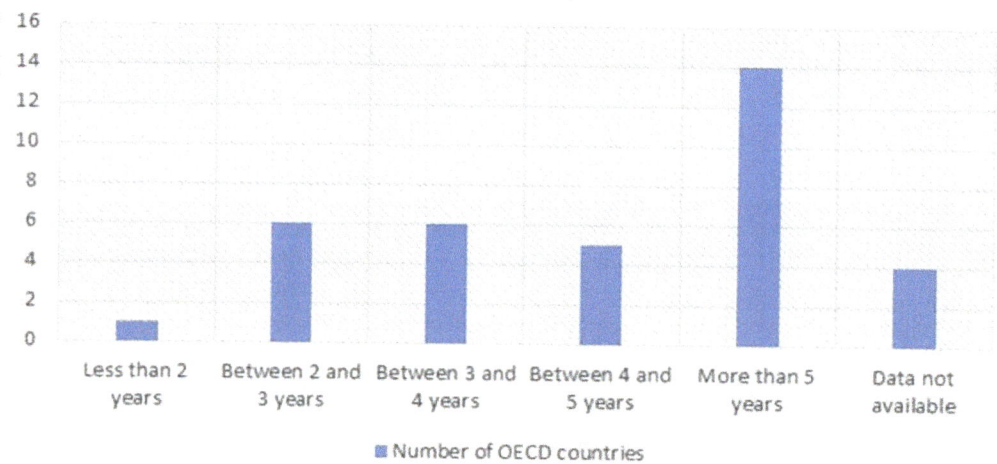

■ Number of OECD countries

Note: Response of 36 OECD countries to Q89: "What is the average length of senior managers' tenure in a particular position?"
Source: OECD (2016), "Strategic Human Resources Management Survey".

In the short term, the dynamics of the relatively high turnover in Brazil's federal administration is likely to have a negative impact on innovation (see, for example, Brandão and Bruno-Faria [2017]). First, the short tenure of senior managers does not give them enough time to understand existing processes and policies. Without this understanding, it is harder to identify priorities, make proposals and design innovative ways of working. Second, when leaders expect their mandate to be relatively short, they have fewer incentives to take a longer term perspective towards the development of their own skills and those of their workforce.

Third, short mandates also affect leaders' perceived legitimacy to lead longer term change initiatives; this lack of long-term vision may affect teams' engagement to work on future-oriented projects such as those requiring innovative and iterative approaches. Finally, turnover of leaders also tends to affect turnover of lower layers of DAS/FCPE positions and other civil servants, because the senior civil servants usually take team members with them when they change positions. Perception from the interviews conducted in Brazil for this report also suggests that civil servants tend to follow a leader that they appreciate, regardless of the sector where they work.

Finally, while intrinsic motivation – such as attachment and engagement towards public sector ethos – is fundamental for long-term sustainability of public policies, it is not clear how the current SCS system could attract leaders based on intrinsic motivation. The relatively high bonuses associated with leadership positions tend to act as extrinsic motivation towards these positions (Instituto República, 2018). In this context, better understanding the incentives that motivate individuals to assume leadership positions should help the federal administration in any future reforms related to improving recruitment to leadership positions.

Findings of the OECD survey on core skills areas for public sector innovation in Brazil

Incorporating change into government functions is one of the most difficult topics facing innovators and public sector leaders in Brazil and elsewhere in the world (OECD, 2018a). To address this challenge, investments in public sector innovation need to start by reconsidering the skills and competencies needed of civil servants and senior officials in public administrations.

There is currently a lack of information about the skills available in the Brazilian civil service. First, most recruitment processes do not formally and systemically assess skills, and second, attempts to map the existing skills in the federal administration are currently at nascent stages. In this context and as part of this report, the OECD conducted a survey to obtain some insights into individual perceptions of skills levels for the six skills areas presented in Chapter 1: iteration, data literacy, user centricity, curiosity, storytelling and insurgency (see Box 2.4).

While the survey is not statistically representative of Brazil's federal administration, the responses from 2 757 people provide useful insights into respondents' perception of innovation skills and opportunities to develop those skills across the federal level. The survey findings, described below and also explored in the Innovation Systems Review (OECD 2019a) conducted in parallel with this report (OECD forthcoming) could possibly be further explored in future studies to understand the abilities and preparedness for public sector innovation.

Box 2.4. OECD survey on the core skills areas for public sector innovation

At Brazil's Innovation Week in November 2018, with the support of the National School of Public Administration (Escola nacional de administração pública, ENAP) and the former Ministry of Planning, the OECD launched a civil service-wide survey to assess respondents' perceptions of their innovation-oriented skills, of management support and of organisational readiness to use the six innovation skills areas identified by the OECD: iteration, data literacy, user-centered, curiosity, storytelling and insurgency.

Each of six innovation skills areas was further divided until subcomponents and participants were asked to rate each subcomponent on a simple three-point scale against three dimensions: 1) their own awareness/proficiency of the skill; 2) encouragement from their manager to use the skill; and 3) their organisation's readiness to adopt the skill. The full list of the subcomponents is available in Table 2.1. A small-scale first pilot of the survey was conducted in Chile in 2016 with a group of 20 public sector innovators from 15 different public institutions and services (OECD, 2017c).

The main objective of the survey was to obtain responses from employees of the federal administration. ENAP sent the survey to its mailing lists and 2 757 people responded. Figure 2.4 shows the profile of those that responded to the survey. Out of the 1 540 respondents from the federal administration, 10% reported themselves as being DAS 4-6 or FCPE 4; 16% as DAS or FCPE 1-3; and 74% as civil servants (non-DAS/FCPE). Twenty-seven respondents did not report belonging to any of these groups.

Figure 2.3. Profile of respondents to the OECD survey

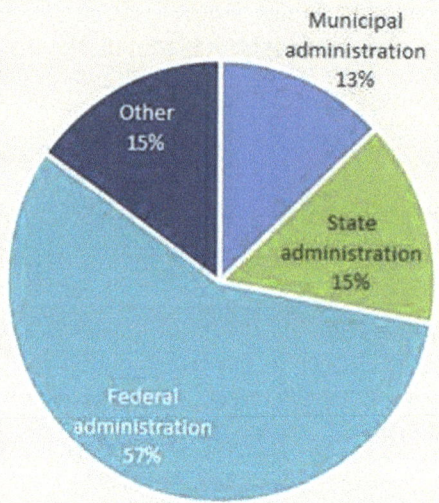

Note: The category "other" includes categories such as universities, the private sector, civil society and the military.
Source: OECD (2018c), "Survey on Innovation Skills: Organisational Readiness Assessment" (Habilidades de Inovação: Avaliação de Prontidão Organizacional), unpublished.

The survey was conducted in Portuguese with a translation provided by ENAP and WeGov. The survey is available in: https://survey2018.oecd.org/Survey.aspx?s=103bc32f2de64776925449ef61fa243a

Overview of the main findings

The results of this survey are based on the individuals who self-reported as working in the federal, state or municipal administrations (2 336 respondents), and more specifically on the people working in the federal administration. Results show that, overall, individuals' self-perception of their own innovation capabilities is higher than their perception of their manager's support and their organisation's readiness. The same findings were observed in the survey conducted in Chile. Interestingly, on average, the perception of their own manager's capacity to support innovation is lower than both the individual skills levels and organisational readiness to use them, including when each administrative level is analysed separately.

When managers' capacity to support innovation in their teams is low, it affects teams' motivation and reduces opportunities to innovate. This result suggests that individuals may feel capable of more innovation than their management is supporting them to achieve – although it is not possible to measure whether individuals are as skilled as they perceive themselves to be. Employees appear to perceive management as unable to build the bridge between organisations and innovators, which would be consistent with the fragmentation of innovation initiatives identified in the Innovation Systems Review (OECD 2019a).

Figure 2.4. Perception of capabilities on innovation skills in the federal, state and municipal administrations

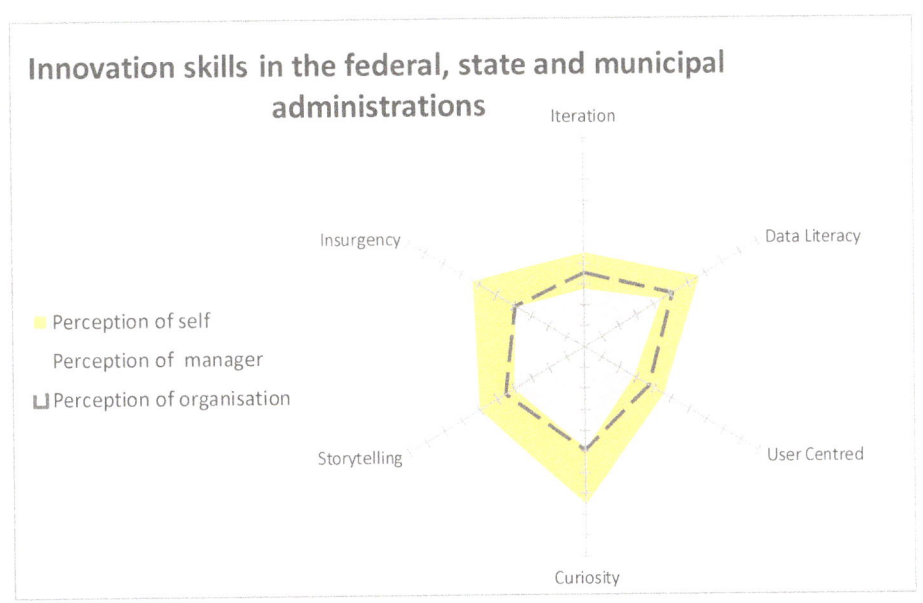

Note: On a scale from 0 to 1. Perception of self: How capable are you in using this skill? 1: I know nothing/very little about this skill; 2: I have a general awareness of this skill; 3: I have a good awareness of this skill/I use it regularly. Perception of manager: How often does your manager support you to use this skill? 1: Not at all/not very often; 2: Occasionally; 3: Very/quite often; Perception of organisation: Is your organisation ready to adopt this skill in its usual way of working? 1: Not at all/not very ready; 2: Somewhat ready/already using it occasionally; 3: Very/quite ready/already using it widely.
Source: OECD (2018c), "Survey on Innovation Skills: Organisational Readiness Assessment" (Habilidades de Inovação: Avaliação de Prontidão Organizacional), unpublished.

Exploring innovation skills and subskills at the federal level

The survey included six skills and 29 subskills as detailed in Table 2.1. The subskills aim to measure concrete aspects of each skill area.

At the federal level, data literacy is the skills area where organisational readiness achieves the highest score. This could reflect Brazil's investment in digital governance through the Digital Governance Strategy (Estratégia de Governança Digital) for the federal administration[13] (Ministry of Planning, Budget and Management [2018], reviewed separately by the OECD [2018b]).

By contrast, user centricity is, with iteration, the skills area where federal employees score themselves the lowest. Strengthening user centricity in the federal administration has been promoted in several official documents as far back as the State Reform of 1995. The reform's "Director Plan" brought the citizen to the core of public value through service delivery and public accountability mechanisms towards civil society (Nassuno, 2000). Improvement of user centricity has also been at the core of many winning innovations in the Innovation in Public Federal Management Competitions.[14] These innovations range from the 1996 innovation to "Improve customer service to tax payers" by the Ministry of Finance[15] to the more recent creation of a web portal which compiles information about the availability of services in municipalities across the country (Mapas Estratégicos para Políticas de Cidadania, MOPS), developed by the former Ministry of Social Development and the Fight against Hunger.[16] Future initiatives to improve user centricity could benefit from further research in this field, especially considering that user centricity remains a criterion in the 2019 Innovation Awards.

Table 2.1. Survey on Innovation Skills: Organisational Readiness Assessment: List of skills and subskills areas

Skills and skill sets	Code
ITERATION (IT)	**IT1**
Using incremental/iterative project management approaches (e.g. agile)	IT 1.1
Using prototypes to develop and explore how different approaches work	IT 1.2
Using experiments to evaluate pilots, projects and policies	IT 1.3
Risk taking and management	IT 1.4
DATA LITERACY (DL)	**DL 2**
Collecting useful, relevant and timely data	DL 2.1
Accessing existing data collected by the government	DL 2.2
Working effectively with analysts and data specialists	DL 2.3
Communicating data analysis and results to non-specialists	DL 2.4
Basing decisions on data and evidence	DL 2.5
USER CENTRED (UX)	**UX 3**
Co-creating solutions with users, involving them throughout the process	UX 3.1
Creating and refining evaluation cycles which regularly collect users' feedback	UX 3.2
Conducting research to find out what users really need from public services	UX 3.3
Facilitating interactive workshops with users to develop or test approaches	UX 3.4
Developing partnerships with organisations that represent users	UX 3.5
Using behavioural science techniques (e.g. "nudge") in public policy	UX3.6
CURIOSITY (CT)	**CT 4**
Asking questions or analysing a situation from different perspectives	CT 4.1
Seeking feedback about how a service can be improved	CT 4.2
Identifying approaches that work elsewhere and adapting them for your own project/team/service	CT 4.3
Working in teams with diverse perspectives and backgrounds	CT 4.4
STORYTELLING (ST)	**ST 5**
Explaining how a project delivers positive changes	ST 5.1
Using multiple methods to communicate project information (e.g. video, infographics, blog posts, etc.)	ST 5.2
Using "user stories" to explain problems or changes from the user's perspective	ST 5.3
Adapting the message as the situation develops or audience changes	ST 5.4
Communicating the results of the project after it is finished to promote learning and diffusion	ST 5.5
INSURGENCY (IN)	**IN 6**
Trying out untested or unusual ways of working, even if they may not work	IN 6.1
Working with new and different partners to deliver projects	IN 6.2
Challenging traditional or default positions and perspectives	IN 6.3
Understanding how the organisation works and how to change it	IN 6.4
Building coalitions to drive change and amplify messages	IN 6.5

Source: OECD (2018c), "Survey on Innovation Skills: Organisational Readiness Assessment" (Habilidades de Inovação: Avaliação de Prontidão Organizacional), unpublished.

By further exploring the individual innovation subskills at the federal level (see Table 2.1 for the full list of subskills), results show that federal employees score themselves the lowest in their capacity to use behavioural sciences. This subskill is part of the skill set "user centricity". Along with the low results of subskill "capability to develop partnerships with organisations that represent users", these contribute to explain why "user centricity" appears as the weakest skill set at the federal level.

Figure 2.5. Mapping innovation skills in Brazil's federal administration

Results of an online survey (n=1 567)

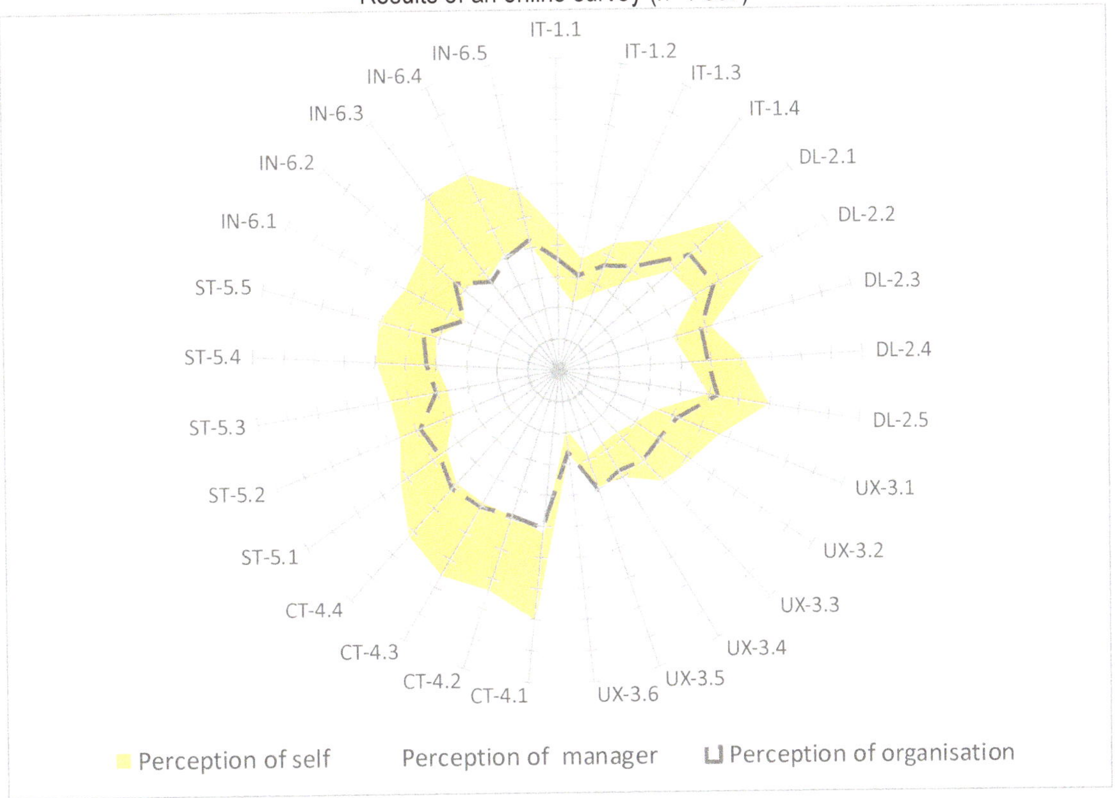

Note: Responses of people who reported working in the federal administration. Skills areas: IT: iteration; DL: data literacy; UX: user centred; CT: curiosity; ST: storytelling; IN: insurgency. See Table 2.1 for the full list of subskills.
Source: OECD (2018c), "Survey on Innovation Skills: Organisational Readiness Assessment" (Habilidades de Inovação: Avaliação de Prontidão Organizacional), unpublished

Within user centricity, the subskill related to user satisfaction is one of the aspects where respondents seem more skilled, possibly because user satisfaction surveys are one of the most traditional methods to interact with users. At the same time, research shows that citizen satisfaction data are not yet widely used across the federal administration (Inova, 2018). The Department for Service Modernisation and Innovation (Inova) of the former Ministry of Planning co-ordinated a survey on federal public service satisfaction, based on the perception of managers and of service users. The preliminary findings on the perception of managers suggest that only in about half the surveyed institutions are users involved in service improvement processes. When asked about the tools available for users to express their satisfaction, only 40% of institutions had such tools, and of these, around 69% use service-user surveys or questionnaires, and only 3.5% report using focus groups (Inova, 2018).

The subskill where federal employees score themselves the highest is the capacity to "ask questions or analyse a situation from different perspectives". The fact that federal employees perceive themselves as highly capable of "understanding different perspectives" could partly explain the low investment on tools to obtain evidence about what those perspectives actually are; for example, using behavioural approaches to understand users' needs. Assumptions about users have a strong potential to bias results, policy design and outcomes. For this reason, a growing number of countries have been using behavioural insights and ethnography to help institutions better design, implement and enhance public policies and market interventions (OECD, 2017a).

Individual perception across hierarchical levels

Looking at the survey results broken down by hierarchical level, curiosity is the skill set where individuals systematically score themselves the highest. Curiosity is also where they consider their manager to be the most supportive. All three hierarchical levels consider data literacy the strongest skill area at organisational level, which is coherent with the previous findings about the potential impact of Brazil's Digital Governance Strategy for the federal government.

The comparison between self-perception at different hierarchical levels suggest that DAS 4-6 and FCPE 4 (i.e. senior managers) perceive themselves as more competent in all of the innovation skill areas than the lower levels of DAS and of civil servants in general. Senior managers also perceive their own managers as more supportive than the two other groups.

Figure 2.6. Innovation skills: Self-perception by hierarchical level

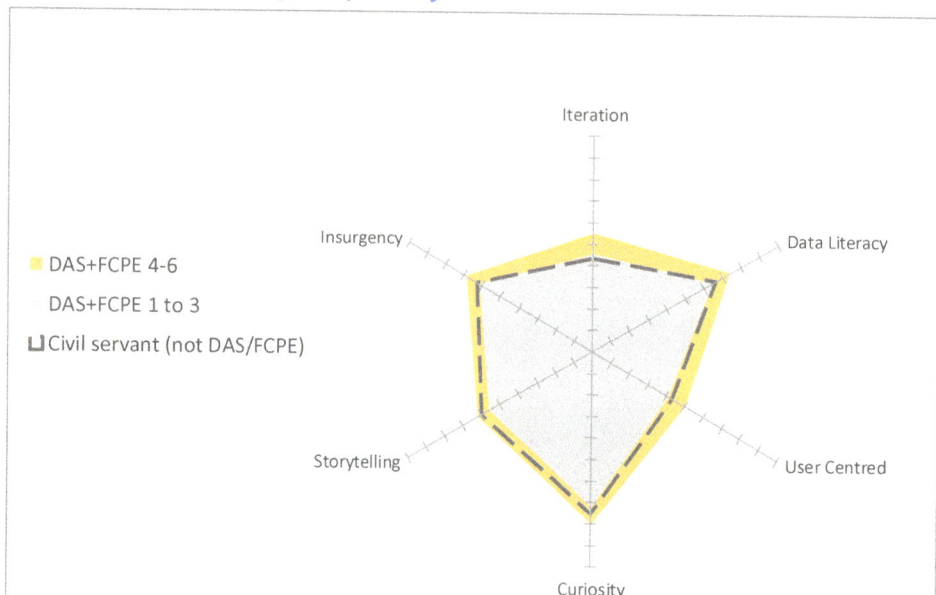

Note: Responses of people who reported working in the federal administration.
Source: OECD (2018c), "Survey on Innovation Skills: Organisational Readiness Assessment" (Habilidades de Inovação: Avaliação de Prontidão Organizacional), unpublished.

Further exploring innovation skills needed in the federal administration

These findings could be relevant to better understand the way managers position themselves in the political-administrative interface. Keeping in mind the limits of the current dataset, further research could investigate whether one possible explanation for senior managers' relatively better perception about their own managers' support could be because their "managers" are the political leaders that appointed them.

Another area for investigation could be the apparent contradiction between how senior managers perceive themselves and how the lower hierarchical levels perceive them. Clearly, senior managers see themselves as more knowledgeable and capable in all six skills areas. However most non-DAS/FCPE civil servants perceive very low support from their managers to use the skills they possess. This gap could be explained by a few phenomenon. For example, it is not clear that the core civil servants report directly to senior managers – and therefore there may be a layer of middle management which is blocking innovative senior leaders from connecting to their innovation-oriented workforce. It may also be due to the difference of perception – senior leaders often perceive more innovation in their organisations than the broader workforce does because senior leaders are more closely placed to it, and may manage it through smaller pockets of specialists removed from the view of the broader public workforce. A similar situation was found in Ireland in the results of the 2017 Employee Engagement Survey, which suggest that the more senior grades feel they have more freedom and space to be innovative than lower grades (Government of Ireland, 2017). In either case, the survey results point to a challenge of engaging the broader workforce in innovation in ways that use their skills to their fullest potential.

Brazil could consider further exploring these baseline findings through employee surveys, a common trend in OECD countries. Among the 30 OECD countries that conduct employee surveys (across the central public administration, by administrative sector or by ministry), 22 use them to assess the effectiveness of management.

Figure 2.7. Focus of employee surveys in OECD countries, 2016

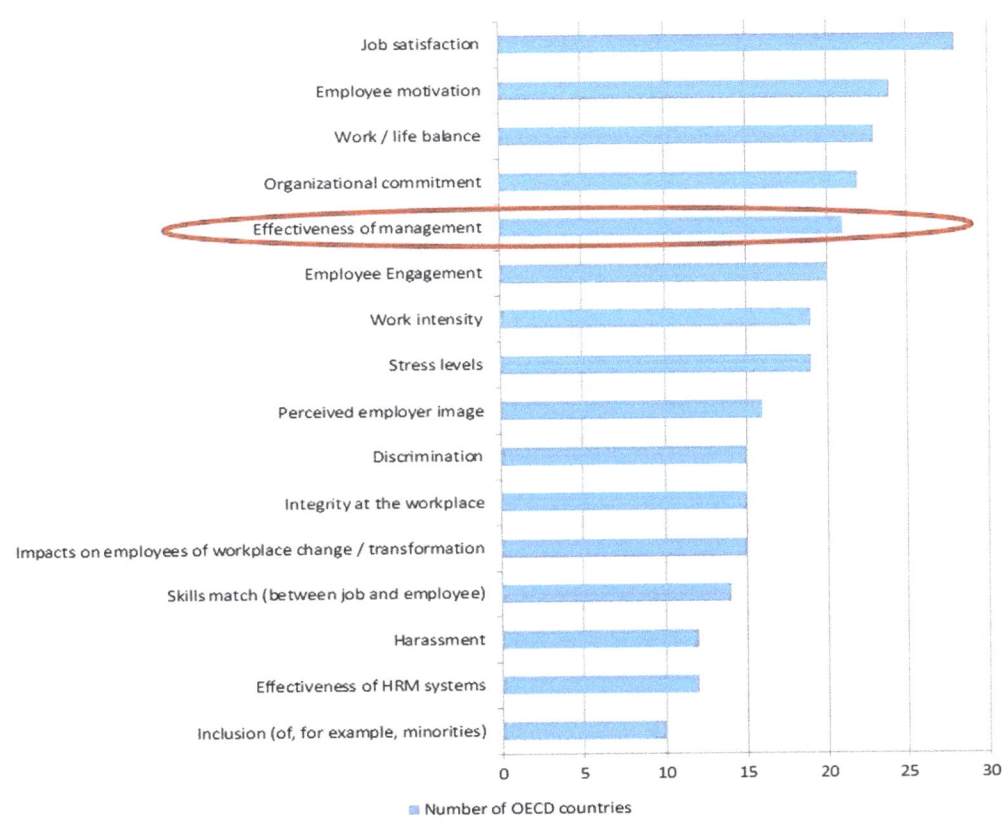

Note: Response of 36 OECD countries to the question: "Q19b: [If you conduct employee surveys,] Do these employee surveys aim to assess the following aspects?"
Source: OECD (2016b), "Strategic Human Resources Management Survey"

This chapter has shown that senior leaders in Brazil find themselves trying to manage and lead a public sector workforce which is highly rigid and fragmented, from an SCS which is itself very flexible. This balance makes it difficult to position learning, development and career progression in a way that can focus on building the workforce needed for innovation in the public sector. It has also shown that many federal public servants perceive significant skills gaps in all aspects of the OECD's six core skills areas for public sector innovation, and don't perceive a great deal of support to use these skills from their management teams. The next chapters look at the three areas of the senior civil service system triangle, to determine the kind of leadership needed in Brazil to address these challenges, and systemic interventions necessary to make it happen.

Notes

[1] Law No. 13.844 of 18 June 2019, Establishing the basic organisation of the Presidency of the Republic and Ministries (Estabelece a organização básica dos órgãos da Presidência da República e dos Ministérios), available at: www.planalto.gov.br/ccivil_03/_Ato2019-2022/2019/Lei/L13844.htm#art74 (assessed 10 July 2019).

[2] A clean reputation and moral suitability have been general criteria for assuming any DAS or FCPE positions, according to Decree No. 9.727 of 15 March 2019 on the criteria, the professional profile and general procedures to fulfil DAS and FCPE positions (Dispõe sobre os critérios, o perfil profissional e os procedimentos gerais a serem observados para a ocupação dos cargos em comissão do Grupo Direção e Assessoramento Superiores – DAS e das *Funções Comissionadas do Poder executivo* –FCPE).

[3] Article 37 of the 1988 Federal Constitution, Constitutional Amendment No. 19, 1998.

[4] Articles 37 and 61 of the 1988 Federal Constitution, §1°, II, a.

[5] Decree No. 5.707 of 2 February 2006.

[6] Decree No. 5.707 of 2 February 2006. See also Article 9 of Law No. 7.834 of 6 October 1989.

[7] Decree No. 9.991 of 28 August 2019, on the National Policy for Staff development available in http://www.planalto.gov.br/ccivil_03/_Ato2019-2022/2019/Decreto/D9991.htm

[8] See Instrução normativa No. 201 of 11 September 2019, available in http://www.in.gov.br/en/web/dou/-/instrucao-normativa-n-201-de-11-de-setembro-de-2019-215812638 (accessed 25 september 2019)

[9] Less than 50% of expected.

[10] Law No. 11784 of 22 September 2008 and Law No. 11907 of 2 February 2009.

[11] Data are not available due to the scattered nature of appointments and dismissals for DAS/FCPE positions.

[12] OECD Strategic Human Resources Management Survey, Q.89: What is the average length of senior managers' tenure in a particular position?

[13] The Digital Governance Strategy defines the strategic objectives, the targets, the indicators and the initiatives of the Digital Government Policy of the Federal Executive (Decree No. 8.638 of 15 January 2016.

[14] For more information about the awards, see: https://inovacao.enap.gov.br/1o-concurso.

[15] Ministério das Finanças.

[16] Ministério do Desenvolvimento Social e Combate à Fome.

References

Brandão, S. and Maria de Fátima Bruno-Faria (2017), "Barreiras à inovação em gestão em organizações públicas do governo federal brasileiro: Análise da percepção de dirigentes", in: ENAP/IPEA (2017), Inovação no Setor Público: Teoria, Tendências e Casos no Brasil, Pedro Cavalcante et al. (orgs.), Brasília, http://repositorio.ipea.gov.br/bitstream/11058/8795/1/Barreiras%20%c3%a0%20inova%c3%a7%c3%a3o .pdf.

Camões, M. and I. Balué (2015), "Análise de processos seletivos para cargos comissionados no âmbito da administração pública federal", VIII Congresso CONSAD de Administração Pública.

Cavalcante, P. and P. Carvalho (2017), "Profissionalização da burocracia federal brasileira (1995-2014): Avanços e dilemas", Revista de Administração Pública, Vol. 51/1, pp. 1-26, http://dx.doi.org/10.1590/0034-7612144002.

Cavalcante, P. and G. Lotta (2015) (orgs), Burocracia de Médio Escalão: Perfil, Trajetória e Atuação, National School of Public Administration, Brasília, http://repositorio.enap.gov.br/bitstream/1/2063/2/Burocratas%20de%20m%c3%a9dio%20escal%c3%a3o .pdf.

ENAP (2018), Informe de Pessoal: Março 2018, National School of Public Administration, Brasília.

Freire, A., P. Cavalcante and P. Palotti (2017), "Perfil e determinantes da ocupação de cargos comissionados no setor de infraestrutura do governo federal no Brasil", in: Paula, J. Et al. (orgs.) (2017), Burocracia Federal de Infraestrutura Econômica: Reflexões sobre Capacidades Estatais, National School of Public Administration and Institute for Applied Economic Research, Brasília.

Government of Ireland (2017), Civil Service: Employee Engagement Survey 2017, prepared by the Department of Public Expenditure and Reform, https://www.gov.ie/pdf/?file=https://assets.gov.ie/3980/071218101844-ff297100dccb400296a8c39fe8feb7f6.pdf#page=1.

Inova (2018), "Pesquisa de Gestão da Qualidade em Serviços Públicos Federais: Resultados preliminares", Department for Service Modernisation and Innovation, www.planejamento.gov.br/cidadania-digital/brasil-eficiente-cidadania-digital/Pesquisa_Gesto_Qualidade_Divulgacao_vFINAL.pdf (accessed 4 April 2019).

Instituto República (2018), "Relatório da 3ª Conferencia Anual do Instituto República '"Serviço Público: Desafios no Brasil'", unpublished.

Lopez, F. and S. Praça (2018), "Cargos de confiança e políticas públicas no executivo federal", in: Pires, R., G. Lotta and V. Elias de Oliveira, Burocracia e Políticas Públicas no Brasil: Interseções Analíticas, Institute for Applied Economic Research and National School of Public Administration, Brasília.

Matheson, A. et al. (2007), "Study on the political involvement in senior staffing and on the delineation of responsibilities between ministers and senior civil servants", OECD Working Papers on Public Governance, No. 6, OECD Publishing, Paris, https://doi.org/10.1787/136274825752

Ministry of Planning, Budget and Management (2018), "Estratégia de Governança Digital (EGD) – Versão Revisitada", Ministry of Planning, Budget and Management, https://www.governodigital.gov.br/EGD.

Nassuno, M. (2000), "A administração com foco no usuário-cidadão: Realizações no governo federal brasileiro nos últimos 5 anos", revised version of a paper presented at the V Congresso do Centro Latino Americano da Administração para o Desenvolvimento, www.reformadagestaopublica.org.br/Terceiros/Autores/Nassuno,Marianne/marianne.pdf (accessed 4 April 2019).

Odelius, C.C. (2010), "Gestão de desempenho profissional: Conhecimento acumulado, características desejadas ao sistema e desafios a superar", in: Pantoja, M.J., M.R. de Souza Camões and S. Trescastro Bergue (orgs.), Gestão de Pessoas: Bases Teóricas e Experiências no Setor Público, National School of Public Administration, Brasilia.

OECD (2019a), The Innovation System of the Public Service of Brazil: An exploration of its past, present and future journey, OECD Publishing, Paris.

OECD (2018a), Embracing Innovation in Government: Global Trends 2018, OECD, Paris, https://www.oecd.org/gov/innovative-government/embracing-innovation-in-government-2018.pdf.

OECD (2018b), Digital Government Review of Brazil: Towards the Digital Transformation of the Public Sector, OECD Digital Government Studies, OECD Publishing, Paris, https://doi.org/10.1787/9789264307636-en.

OECD (2018c), "Survey on Innovation Skills: Organisational Readiness Assessment" (Habilidades de Inovação: Avaliação de Prontidão Organizacional), unpublished.

OECD (2017a), Behavioural Insights and Public Policy: Lessons from Around the World, OECD Publishing, Paris, http://dx.doi.org/10.1787/9789264270480-en.

OECD (2017b), Government at a Glance 2017, OECD Publishing, Paris, http://dx.doi.org/10.1787/gov_glance-2017-en.

OECD (2017c), Innovation Skills in the Public Sector: Building Capabilities in Chile, OECD Public Governance Reviews, OECD Publishing, Paris, http://dx.doi.org/10.1787/9789264273283-en.

OECD (2016a), Government at a Glance Latin America and the Caribbean 2017, OECD Publishing, Paris, http://dx.doi.org/10.1787/888933431042.

OECD (2016b), "Strategic Human Resources Management Survey", OECD, Paris.

OECD (2010), OECD Reviews of Human Resource Management in Government: Brazil 2010: Federal Government, OECD Reviews of Human Resource Management in Government , OECD Publishing, Paris, https://doi.org/10.1787/9789264082229-en.

Palotti, P. and A. Freire (2015), Perfil, Composição e Remuneração dos Servidores Públicos Federais: Trajetória Recente e Tendências Observadas, Cadernos ENAP, No. 42: Servidores públicos federais: Novos Olhares e Perspectivas, National School of Public Administration, Brasilia.

Pinheiro, I.A. (2017), Em Busca da Congruência entre o Ambiente (à Luz das Demandas da Sociedade), as Estruturas e a Gestão dos Cargos e Carreiras no Setor Público, ENAP Cadernos, No. 49, National School of Public Administration, Brasilia.

Secretary of Management (2018), Integrated System for Staff Administration (Sistema Integrado de Administração de Pessoal, SIAPE).

Weber, A. (2012), "Alta dirección pública", presentation given at the seminar Fortaleciendo la Capacidad del Empleo Público Colombiano, Bogota, 27 July 2012.

3. Key skills for innovative leaders in Brazil's federal administration

This chapter maps the evolution of public sector leadership competencies, arguing that the call for public sector innovation requires leadership that is not only transformational, but also horizontal and distributed. It then presents the concept of leadership competency frameworks, illustrated by various examples used in many OECD countries. It then identifies the types of skills, mindsets and behaviours that leaders need to support innovation in the Brazilian context, based on insights from public servants and in the federal administration.

Chapter 1 built a case for the need to ensure high-quality leadership in Brazil to support a more productive, effective and innovative public service. Innovation cannot be successful without support from public leaders with the right skills, competencies and styles. Effective leaders mobilise and engage staff to promote desired outcomes, and ensure that employees have the right resources and opportunities to use their skills and drive positive change in their organisations.

The OECD survey presented in Chapter 2 finds a public service in Brazil that has some of the skills necessary to innovate, yet, innovation is not happening at the level needed or expected. The concurrent Innovation Systems review conducted by the OECD's Observatory for Public Sector Innovation (OPSI) mirrors these findings (OECD 2019). The challenge for Brazil's public leaders is to find ways of activating the full potential of the innovative talent that resides within their organisations. In the OECD's discussions with Brazilian civil servants, leadership was one of the most cited reasons for both success and failure of innovation. The ability of senior civil servants to lead and drive innovation is therefore a strong determinant of successful innovation in Brazil. This chapter identifies leaders' competencies for innovation by highlighting the characteristics of successful public sector leaders in a Brazilian context.

Evolution of the public sector leader

In the public sector, the practice of studying, defining and attempting to replicate good leadership was formalised in the 1980s and 1990s through competency-based leadership. Over the past 20 years, there has been an evolution in the understanding and expectation of public sector leadership, reflected in the competency models of senior civil service (SCS) systems in many OECD countries. While a "tough-talking, take-charge, individualistic view of public leadership is alive and well through the world" (Crosby and Bryson, 2018), there is growing evidence and academic rigour that identifies necessary alternatives to "heroic" models of public leadership. These alternatives recognise that public sector innovation cannot be successful if it is singularly driven or controlled by one leader from the top. Rather, these models focus on groups of leaders, both hierarchical and situational, that can successfully drive innovation together.

Sometimes called "adaptive", "pragmatic" or "distributed" leadership, these models emphasise an "anti-hero" form of leadership. An anti-hero adapts his/her leadership style according to circumstances. Anti-hero leaders are aware of the limitations of their own knowledge and skills and build expertise among their followers, which they can rely on to complement their own expertise. This suggests that a leader in the context of public sector innovation should have a lower perception of their own innovation skills than those of the workforce they build around them, rather than the other way around, as appears to be the case in Brazil's federal administration (see Chapter 2). The five pillars of anti-heroic leadership – empathy, humility, flexibility, acknowledgement of uncertainty and self-awareness – are helpful for thinking about the leadership styles necessary to build and support innovation capabilities within public sector organisations (Wilson, 2013).

Despite great interest among academics and public sector practitioners, the practise of distributed leadership in the public sector is quite nascent. Early in their adoption, distributed leadership models described the complex governance environments where true change requires co-ordinated leadership across multiple organisations which are not hierarchically organised. However, these are often difficult to implement within public sector organisations as they are not well aligned with traditional public sector hierarchies and accountably structures. These traditional heroic models are reinforced by oversight and audit organisations which enforce the traditional and current public sector accountability models, which view accountability as an individual activity, generally concentrated at the top.

A related strand of the public sector leadership debate revolves around values-based and ethical leadership. Values-driven culture and leadership is the first pillar of the OECD Recommendation of the Council on Public Sector Leadership and Capability. Values guide the judgement of public servants, including leaders, on how to perform their tasks in daily operations. The Recommendation acknowledges that specific values vary across countries, but common values include accountability, integrity, the rule of law and serving in the public interest.

Values-based leaders usually display a high degree of self-awareness, and are able to draw on and leverage the values of their colleagues as a motivating factor for both themselves and their teams. These values are ideally articulated in a structured way and used to guide decision making. Values-based leadership relates to two interconnected elements – a leaders' own values, which they understand and use to make effective decisions – and a leaders' ability to promote values in their workplace and inspire values-based behaviour among their followers (Treviño, Hartman and Brown, 2000).

Public sector leadership competency models

Leadership competencies are clear statements about the skills and behaviours that a government expects from its leadership cadre. When integrated into human resources processes, they become powerful strategic tools to guide decisions about leadership appointments, development, performance and accountability. Some OECD countries have actively used leadership competencies for decades, and they are now actively used in most OECD countries, as shown in Figure 3.1 (OECD, 2016).

Figure 3.1. Existence of a competency framework that enables a classification of skills and competencies for senior managers (leadership competencies)

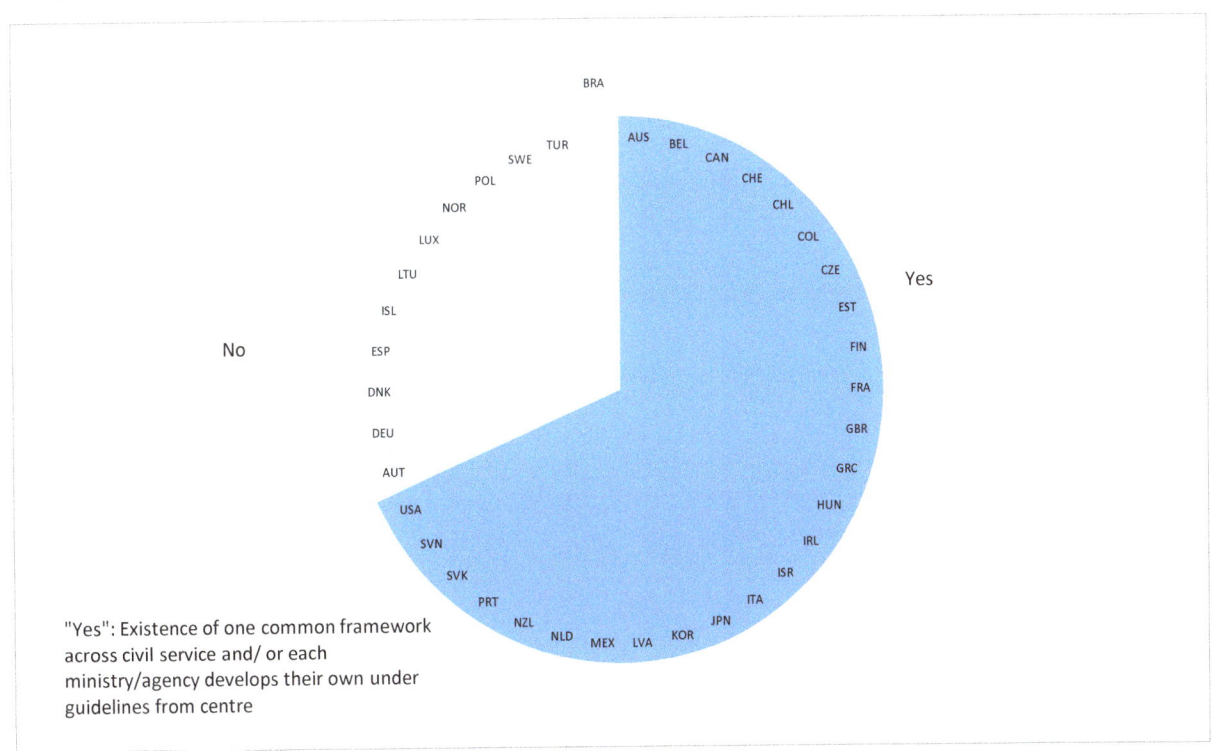

Source: OECD (2016), "Strategic Human Resources Management Survey", Question Q25. Is there a common skills inventory/competency framework that enables a classification of skills and competencies? Data for Brazil based on interviews.

The United States, whose senior leadership contains a mix of politically appointed and career civil servants, has developed a model with "five executive core qualifications"[1]:

Leading change: The ability to bring about strategic change, both within and outside the organisational goals. The ability to establish an organisational vision and to implement it in a continuously changing environment.

- **Leading people**: The ability to lead people toward meeting the organisation's vision, mission and goals. The ability to provide an inclusive workplace that fosters the development of others, facilitates co-operation and teamwork, and supports constructive resolution of conflicts.

- **Results driven**: The ability to meet organisational goals and customer expectations. The ability to take decisions that produce high-quality results by applying technical knowledge, analysing problems and calculating risks.

- **Business acumen**: the ability to manage human, financial and information resources strategically.

- **Building coalitions**: The ability to build coalitions internally (i.e. intra- and inter-ministerial partnerships) and with other federal agencies, state and local governments, non-profit and private sector organisations, foreign governments, or international organisations to achieve common goals.

Additionally, each of the core qualifications has sub-components[2] to provide greater clarity and nuance to the qualifications. This framework is used during hiring, selection and evaluation of both politically appointed and career senior leadership positions other than heads of agencies, who are vetted and approved by Congress.

In 2017, Estonia released its new leadership competency model, made up of six core competencies for leaders, specifically referencing innovation, designing for the future, achieving results and empowering others. "The 2017 competence model for the top civil service describes a leader who is a bold designer of the future, an achiever, an inspiring driver of innovation, a genuine value builder for target groups and an effective self-leader."[3]

Figure 3.2. Estonia's leadership competency model

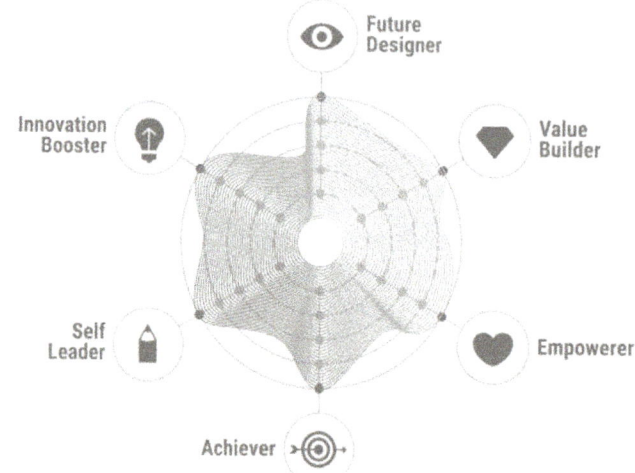

Source: Estonian Government (2017), "Competency framework", https://www.riigikantselei.ee/en/supporting-government/top-executives-civil-service/competency-framework.

Chile also uses leadership competencies (Figure 3.3). Its Senior Executive Service System comprises 1 557 positions, or approximately 30% of the workforce, in the central government. Created in 2003, the Senior Executive Service System was developed to create a process of modernisation and transparency based around merit-based hiring decisions and open competition.

Figure 3.3. Chile's Senior Executive Service System profile

Profile of senior civil servants for Chile

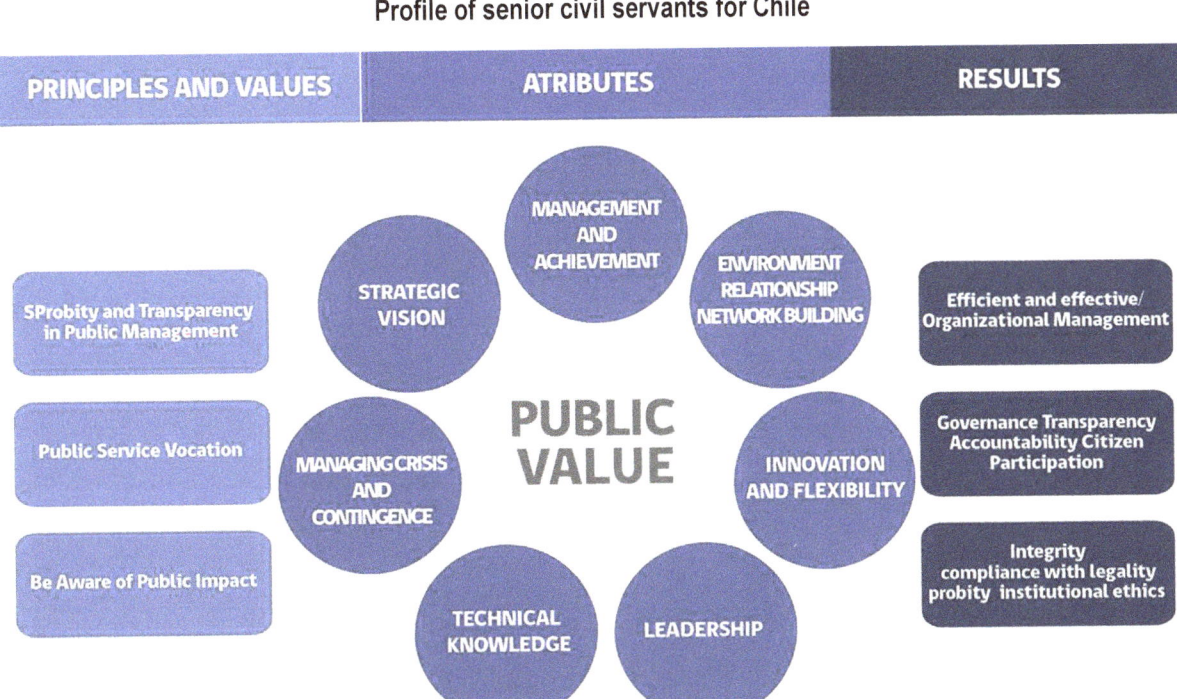

Source: Servicio Civil, 2018

By developing and using profiles that focus on principles and values, attributes, and results as well as using an open merit-based process, the Chilean government received an average of 117 applications per position in 2017. As a result of moving to a profile-based recruitment system, Chile now has 28% of managers from the private sector, 29% are women (previously women comprised only 23.5%), and a strong cadre of future leaders that can use the profile to focus on specific training and experiences.

In Brazil, competencies for senior leaders have been at the heart of discussions about the quality of public management, within and outside the federal administration. The civil society organisation Vetor Brasil uses a competency-based approach to help municipalities and states recruit their leaders (see Chapter 5). Civil society stakeholders are also reflecting on the opportunities and challenges of applying competency-based approaches to the recruitment and development of public managers. Discussions at the Instituto República's 3rd Annual Conference on Challenges for the Public Sector (2018) highlighted the need to map skills and skills gaps, which tend to happen when people assume new positions, particularly management (Instituto República, 2018). The Dom Cabral Foundation has also developed a competency model for public managers (mapa das competências gerenciais), which looks at innovation skills needed from a strategic perspective, specific for senior managers, middle managers and line managers (Figure 3.4) (Fundação Dom Cabral 2018).

Figure 3.4. Managerial behaviours for innovation (extract)

Selected features from the Dom Cabral Foundation's map of competencies

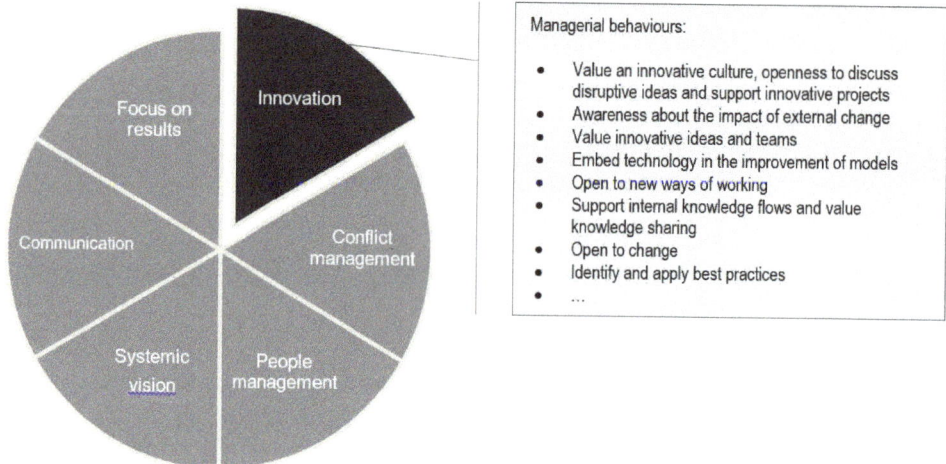

Managerial behaviours:

- Value an innovative culture, openness to discuss disruptive ideas and support innovative projects
- Awareness about the impact of external change
- Value innovative ideas and teams
- Embed technology in the improvement of models
- Open to new ways of working
- Support internal knowledge flows and value knowledge sharing
- Open to change
- Identify and apply best practices
- …

Source: Fundação Dom Cabral (2018)

Innovative leadership competencies for Brazil's federal administration

As the Brazilian public sector continues to focus on driving results and public value for the country, it aims ensure sustainability through a strong, robust and flexible leadership cadre and pipeline of future leaders. One strategy to improve the development, hiring and assessment of current and future leaders is by identifying a group of competencies that reflects the skills needed to innovate in the public sector today and succeed in the future.

The National School of Public Administration (Escola nacional de administração pública, ENAP) was one of the first public sector institutions in Brazil to create a leadership competency model that includes innovation as a core competency.

Figure 3.5. National School of Public Administration's leadership competency model

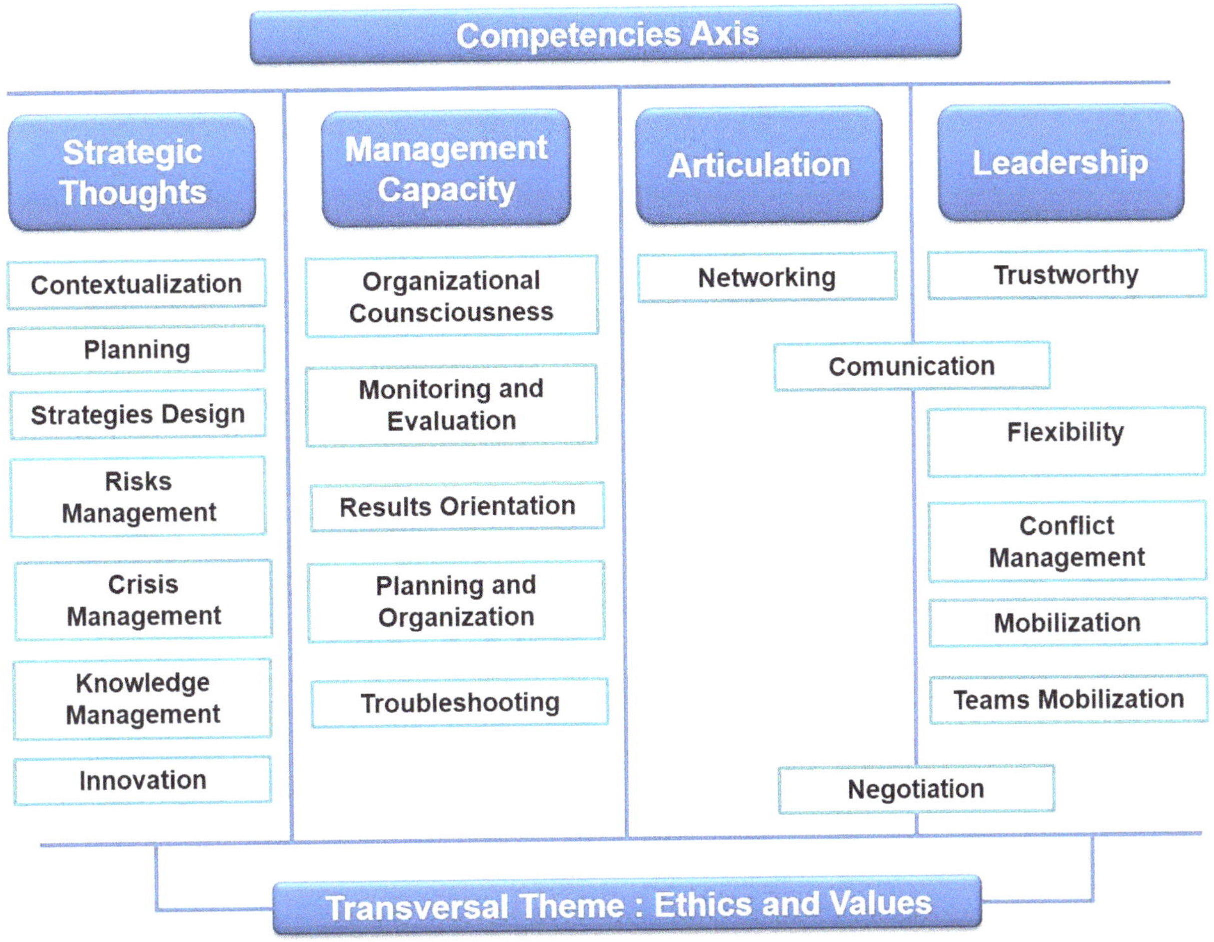

Source: ENAP (2010), "Desenvolvimento de competências de direção: A experiência da Escola Nacional de Administração Pública".

The competencies discussed below and shown in Figure 3.6 are built on the foundation of ENAP's model and input from Brazilian civil servants involved in innovation provided during the course of the OECD's interviews and workshops. They are also built upon good practices around the world and leading literature on public sector leadership. These competencies can be taken into consideration alongside existing competency frameworks in Brazil in order to develop a framework tailored to the context of the Brazilian public sector.

Figure 3.6. Leadership for innovation, an initial model for Brazil's civil service

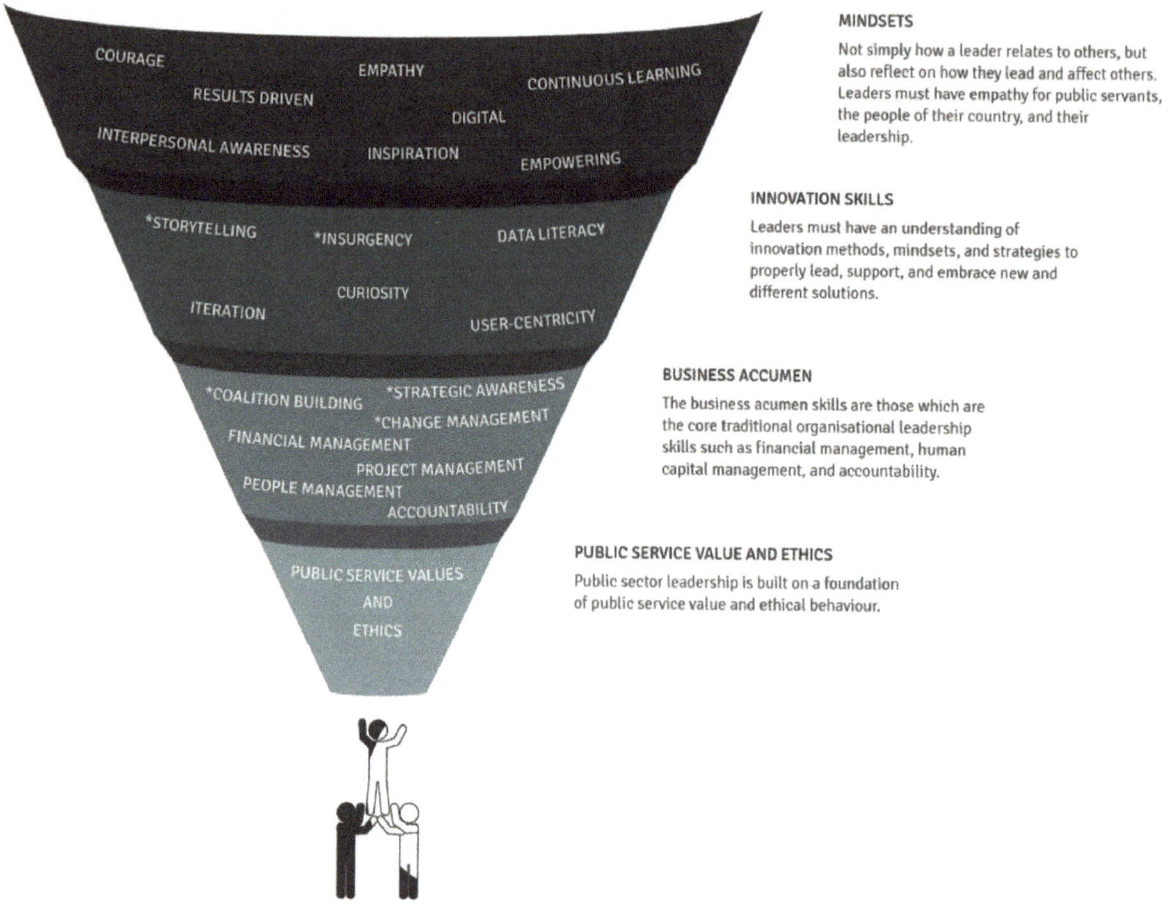

MINDSETS

Not simply how a leader relates to others, but also reflect on how they lead and affect others. Leaders must have empathy for public servants, the people of their country, and their leadership.

INNOVATION SKILLS

Leaders must have an understanding of innovation methods, mindsets, and strategies to properly lead, support, and embrace new and different solutions.

BUSINESS ACCUMEN

The business acumen skills are those which are the core traditional organisational leadership skills such as financial management, human capital management, and accountability.

PUBLIC SERVICE VALUE AND ETHICS

Public sector leadership is built on a foundation of public service value and ethical behaviour.

Source: Author's design

The competencies above are divided into three distinct, but interconnected groups: 1) innovation skills; 2) business acumen; and 3) mindsets; sitting on a foundation of ethics and public service values which guide decision making towards the public interest. Building on this foundation, leadership needs business acumen competencies to manage the business of their department, recognising that these competencies often differ in specific and important ways between the private and public sectors, and even among different public sector organisations. Moving to the next section, leaders need at least a solid understanding of the six innovation skills areas presented in Chapter 1 and measured in Chapter 2. Lastly the effectiveness of a leader and the ability to harness a leader's and an organisation's competencies is dependent on the mental approach, or mindsets, of the leader.

Certain competencies in the business acumen and innovation section have been marked with an asterisk (*). This is to denote that, as a baseline, leaders should have stronger knowledge of and experience with these skills. To help define a leader's ability within each competency, the model views skills on a continuum:

1. aware: general understanding of the practice and how it applies to leading the public sector
2. capable: being able to use the skill and understanding its application
3. Specialised: adopting these skills in the leader's day-to-day use and applying them in a more strategic and systematic way.

An individual leader should not be expected to be an expert in each competency, as doing so would reinforce the hero view of leadership and set unrealistic expectations that would disqualify strong potential candidates. Rather, a nuanced view of competencies should be job-specific to allow for flexibility while also ensuring that minimally, leaders are "aware" in each competency and "capable" in the most critical competency areas. For example, a chief information officer vacancy will likely require a "specialised" rating in skills such as iteration and digital.

Ethics and public service values

Values and ethics exist as a social contract between the government and citizens. As the Brazilian public sector continues to focus on rooting out corruption, there is a clear need to make ethics and values explicit within any competency model. This can be done by framing ethical considerations in a clearly articulated set of public service values. While such values may vary by country, commonly stated values in OECD countries' public services include accountability, impartiality, the rule of law, integrity, transparency, equality and inclusiveness.

Research on ethical leadership suggests that there are two important aspects to ethical leadership (Treviño, Hartman and Brown, 2000). First, the leader should be ethical themselves – this means they have a clear understanding of their values and those of their organisation, and they use these to guide their decision-making processes. Second, they need skills to impart ethical decision making down throughout the organisation they lead. This implies that they need be seen by others as taking values-based decisions, and they need to support others to follow these values when taking their own decisions. This suggests a need to ensure distributed leadership, relying on common values to guide the collective rather than a specific individual. This should therefore improve the collective ethical actions of the group (Van Wart, 2011).

Another finding from the ethical leadership literature is that developing values-based leadership is a long-term goal rather than a competency that is easily learnt. Recent research suggests that ethical leadership does not start once one is a leader. Rather, the primary influence on the ethics of leaders is their own managers and leaders during the early stages of their career (Brown and Treviño, 2006). As such, developing values-based leadership and organisational culture is never finished. This is why the first pillar of the OECD's 2019 Recommendation of the Council on Public Service Leadership and Capability calls for values-driven culture and leadership in the public service, centred on improving outcomes for society.

Brazil has a number of recent documents on ethics and values that have shaped some of the current discourse around leadership, innovation and change in the public sector. In 1994, Decree No. 1171 – Professional Ethics of the Public Civil Servant of the Federal Executive Branch – was put into law (Casa Civil, 1994). The decree outlined 15 pieces of deontological ethical guidance. The last two pieces of guidance made explicit the core functions and prohibitions of public servants, liking ethical behaviour to efficient service provision. In 2007, Decree No. 6029 formalised and centralised the review of ethical standards by creating a Public Ethics Commission.

Box 3.1. Values-driven leadership and culture in the OECD's Recommendation of the Council on Public Service Leadership and Capability

The first pillar of the OECD Recommendation of the Council on Public Service Leadership and Capability calls for a values-driven culture and leadership in the public service, centred on improving outcomes for society. In the context of this Recommendation, "values" refers to core organisational values that guide the judgement of public servants in how to perform their tasks in daily operations. While such values may vary by system, commonly stated core public values include accountability, impartiality, the rule of law, integrity, transparency, equality and inclusiveness. The first principle of this Recommendation is that countries:

Define the values of the public service and promote values-based decision making, in particular through:

1. clarifying and communicating the shared fundamental values which should guide decision making in the public service

2. demonstrating accountability and commitment to such values through behaviour and

3. providing regular opportunities for all public servants to have frank discussions about values, their application in practice and the systems in place to support values-based decision making.

Source: OECD (2019b), Recommendation of the Council on Public Service Leadership and Capability, https://legalinstruments.oecd.org/en/instruments/OECD-LEGAL-0445 (accessed 4 April 2019).

During the OECD's discussions with innovators and leaders conducted as part of this review, the OECD observed that most conversations around ethics focused on prohibitive actions and compliance, rather than on the ethical principles themselves. This narrative centred on explicit expectations and prohibitive activities, results in a heightened sense of risk and an immediate concern of protecting an individual's career by avoiding many of the ambiguities that can stem from the intersection of laws, values and ethics. The guiding principles of conduct appear to be increasingly compliance and fear-based rather than motivational and values-based. When personal protection takes precedent over proactively serving society, the civil service often resorts to retrenchment to protect the status quo without recognition that the status quo can also be doing harm. This situation appears to be reinforced by the career system (see Chapter 2), which many suggest creates a competition that prioritises the status quo.

In order for a foundation of values and ethics to shape the culture for both leaders and civil servants, the focus of work needs to shift towards citizen interests. When the system skews towards heavy punishment, ambiguity can cause inaction.

In 1999, Australia developed a Code of Conduct as part of the Public Service Act. This Code of Conduct set forth basic requirements and expectations of employees. Additionally, the Public Service Act also developed the "APS Values" as additional mandatory standards of behaviour.

Figure 3.7. Australian Public Service values

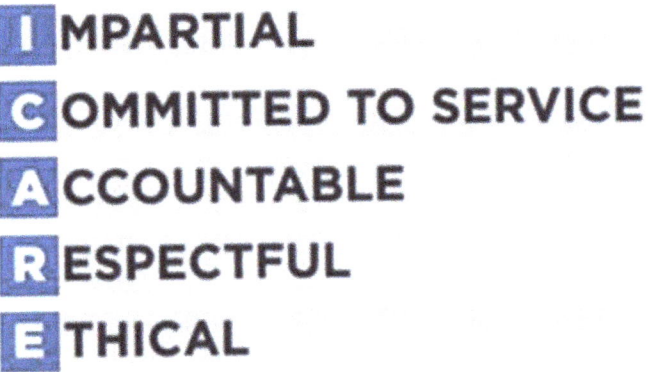

Source: Copyright, Australian Public Service Commission (2018)

In the Australian Public Service Commission's State of the Service Report 2017-18, an ethical review of employees potentially in breach of these mandatory standards occurred with 569 employees – or the equivalent of 0.4% of the civil service – a three-year low.

Just as interesting, the Australian Public Service Commission also uses the report to look at how well the values are being implemented and influencing the culture of the Australian Public Service.

Source: Australian Public Service Commission (2018), State of the Service Report 2017-18, https://www.apsc.gov.au/sites/default/files/18583_-_apsc_-_sosr_-_web.pdf

Business acumen

The business acumen competencies are traditional organisational management competencies such as financial management, people management and accountability.

Within this area, three critical competencies require greater focus and experience: 1) change management; 2) strategic awareness/political savvy; and 3) coalition building. As discussed in Chapter 1, guiding an organisation through change is a key requirement of modern public sector leadership. Leaders must be able to be flexible, adapt and guide organisations through ambiguity and complexity.

To manage change, leaders must also have a strong grasp of the political environment within both their organisation and the system-at-large. This also requires building coalitions and moving from an organisational perspective to a systems perspective (Crosby and Bryson, 2018). Therefore, achieving results is not an individual activity, but a collaborative process leading to shared outcomes among agencies and sectors, and greater democratic accountability to ensure responsiveness and inclusiveness (Van Wart, 2013).

In OECD workshops with public servants, there appeared to be agreement that the business acumen competencies of senior management are the strongest of the three included in the model. Because these are more tangible and better understood, management training is often dedicated to these competencies and promotion opportunities stem from one's ability in business acumen.

However, many of these business acumen competencies change in the context of innovation. For example, the concept of project management has continued to evolve with governments increasingly focused on the delivery of products and services. The need to understand modern approaches to more agile forms of project and product management is critical for leaders to manage teams, high-priority initiatives and accountability. Agile project management is also one of the skill sets with the lowest reported usage according the OECD survey on innovation skills presented in Chapter 2. Likewise, traditional budget management becomes more challenging when dealing with iterative processes and remains one of the common barriers to citizen-centred activities which require collaboration across institutional (and budgetary) silos.

Box 3.3. The difference between leadership and management

In discussions about public sector leadership, it is often assumed that the "manager" of a team is also the "leader" of the team. Managers of teams, organisations and ministries are expected to be both proficient managers and leaders to the point that the terms are generally used interchangeable. If managers were all proficient leaders, innovation would likely be occurring at a higher level than it is today in Brazil. Therefore, it is important to differentiate the terms and their implications.

Even in origin, manager and leader have different meanings. The modern day definition of leader stems from an old English term "to be first." Meanwhile, manager has its roots in Italian and French, and the French word, ménager, means "to keep house."

Managers provide process oversight and keep things running smoothly. In terms of the Brazilian public sector, managers appear to focus first and foremost on documenting activities that auditing organisations require so as to prove that each step was followed in a defined process. This activity becomes the core driver for managers – valuing the checkbox of activities over attempting to inspire and lead.

As William Saito, special adviser from the Cabinet Office of Japan, stated in the 2015 OECD Idea Factory: "In the age of rapid innovation, it is important to distinguish between leadership and management... Today we really need leadership. While managers are needed to optimise mass production and cost reduction, leadership is needed for the rapid rate of innovation. Companies need to hire for leadership qualities, such as constantly doing new things and not being afraid to fail."

Therefore, the challenge is not developing managers, but elevating the current and future public sector managers into public sector leaders. This requires a great focus on the development of innovation skills and mindsets while maintaining and reviewing the strong standard already established for business acumen in light of innovation in the public sector.

Source: OECD IdeaFactory (2015), "Shaping our future leaders", https://www.oecd.org/forum/about/OECD-2015-IdeaFactory-Shaping-Our-Future-Leaders.pdf.

Innovation skills

In 2017, the Observatory of Public Sector Innovation (OPSI) developed "The six core skills areas of public sector innovation" (see Figure 1.4 in Chapter 1) based on insights from innovators around the world (OECD, 2017).

The skills model is intended to help individual civil servants become practitioners, and to ensure that leaders gain an understanding of innovation methods, mindsets and strategies to properly lead, support and embrace new and different solutions. By having a stronger understanding of innovation skills, leaders are able to provide the space and resources necessary for divergent ideas to be explored and tested. Without such an understanding, leaders can unintentionally undermine their organisation's potential to use innovation skills, processes, methodologies or solutions.

As with business acumen, leaders should be more capable in some skills areas. During the OECD's missions to Brazil, a leader's ability to "win hearts and minds" and "articulate a vision" was seen as extremely important to current Brazilian public sector innovators. Many Brazilian public servants used the term "communication" to encapsulate the gap, but communication is a broad term that often translates into simply increasing the volume of talking or e-mails without increasing understanding, building empathy or creating coalitions.

Rather, public sector leaders should be strong storytellers. Storytelling can be defined as communications with empathy. Storytelling does not simply mean being an expert orator, but rather, explaining a vision, priority, change or initiative in a way that builds support. This requires leaders to understand their audience's priorities, values, experiences and feelings to effectively deliver a message regardless of the medium.

Finally, as leaders drive, lead and make space for innovation, they themselves need to show a strong ability to challenge the status quo. This requires skills related to political process and timing, legal understanding to clarify areas where innovation is possible, and the ability to build new and different coalitions that allow for novel and divergent thinking. The OECD calls this skill set "insurgency".

Mindsets

In the OECD's discussions with leaders and innovators in Brazil, the mindsets of public sector leaders were the most cited factor in determining a successful innovative leader. They were also cited as the largest gap in Brazilian senior leadership.

While mindsets are usually listed as core competencies in many public sector leadership models, they are rarely tested, assessed and valued as much as technical competencies due to the lack of assessment tools.

Mindsets shape culture, values and experiences in the public sector. If leaders show they do not value a digital mindset, most digital projects are likely to fail due to a lack of leadership support (i.e. allocating the necessary resources, training employees in digital skills or helping teams overcome bureaucratic challenges) regardless of the demands of civil society. Therefore, without the proper focus on the mindsets of the public sector, good employees become disengaged or leave, new ideas are not generated, and progress stalls.

Additionally, many of these mindsets are necessary for successful implementation of innovation skills or business acumen. For instance, a leader will struggle to achieve results without having a clear vision, driving the change necessary to achieve that vision and communicating the vision appropriately. This also relates to a leader's ability to be inspiring. Leaders who can collectively develop and sell a vision and inspire others are more likely to achieve results, see innovative ideas flow throughout the organisation and improve the value of the public sector.

Based on the OECD Digital Government Review of Brazil, the OECD recommends leaders also be equipped with a digital mindset. This does not mean that a leader must be fluent in digital technologies, but rather, that leaders, even in non-technical positions, must have an understanding of why digital is critical to any government solution and incorporate digital thinking into change processes as early as possible (OECD, 2018b).

Mindsets are not simply how a leader relates to others, but also reflect how they lead and affect others. Leaders must have a deep empathy for public servants, the people of Brazil and their own leadership. By having an understanding of the people that are part of their system, they also gain a greater interpersonal awareness whereby leaders understand how their actions, attitudes and demands impact others.

Mindsets are becoming more critical to the definition of good leadership in the public service. Certain mindsets were already listed in the Estonian and US models. Additionally, in 2014 the United Kingdom emphasised how critical mindsets were to leadership by releasing a Civil Service Leadership Statement (Figure 3.9).

Figure 3.8. UK Civil Service Leadership Statement

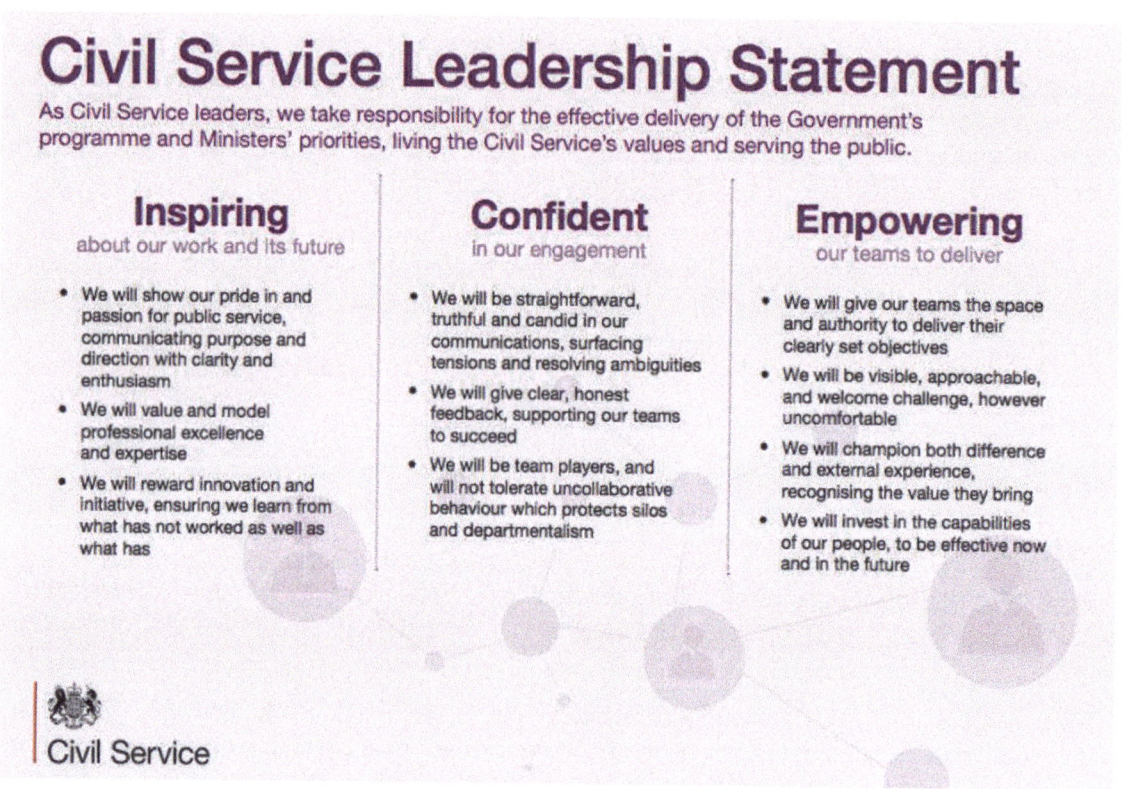

Source: UK Cabinet Office. For more information about the UK Civil Service Leadership Statement, see: https://www.gov.uk/government/publications/civil-service-leadership-statement/civil-service-leadership-statement.

This statement reflects the importance of mindsets to delivering public value by emphasising that inspiring, confident and empowering are the three most critical roles and expectations of leaders.

Identifying the needed leadership competencies in Brazil's senior levels is only the first step towards consistently deploying these skills. OECD countries increasingly develop policies, processes, systems and tools to ensure that their senior leaders have the abilities, motivations and opportunities needed to drive innovation and lead change. The emergence of senior civil service systems in many OECD countries aims to develop the supply of, and ensure demand for, the types of competencies discussed in this chapter. Chapter 4 looks at how some initiatives are emerging in Brazil's federal public service to build the supply of such competencies through the development of current and potential future leaders. Taking into account that developing this supply of competencies will not achieve results if there no demand for them, Chapter 5 looks at what more needs to be done to build the demand for these competencies among those who take appointment decisions for these positions, and hold them accountable for performance.

Notes

[1] For more information, see: https://www.opm.gov/policy-data-oversight/senior-executive-service/executive-core-qualifications.

[2] For more about the US Office of Personnel Management executive core qualifications, see: https://www.hks.harvard.edu/educational-programs/executive-education/admissions-fees/executive-core-qualifications.

[3] For more information about Estonia's competency model, see: https://riigikantselei.ee/en/supporting-government/top-executives-civil-service/competency-framework.

References

Australian Public Service Commission (2018), State of the Service Report 2017-18, Commonwealth of Australia, https://www.apsc.gov.au/sites/default/files/18583_-_apsc_-_sosr_-_web.pdf.

Brown, M. and L. Treviño (2006), "Ethical leadership: A review and future directions", Leadership Quarterly, Vol. 17/6, pp. 595 616, http://dx.doi.org/10.1016/j.leaqua.2006.10.004.

Casa Civil (1994), Decreto No. 1.171, de 22 de Junho de 1994 que Aprova o Código de Ética Profissional do Servidor Público Civil do Poder Executivo Federal, www.planalto.gov.br/ccivil_03/decreto/d1171.htm.

Crosby, B.C. and J.M. Bryson (2018), "Why leadership of public leadership research matters: And what to do about it", Public Management Review, Vol. 20/9, pp. 1264-1286, https://doi.org/10.1080/14719037.2017.1348731.

ENAP (2010), "Desenvolvimento de competências de direção: A experiência da Escola Nacional de Administração Pública", National School of Public Administration, Brasilia.

Estonian Government (2017), "Competency framework", webpage, https://www.riigikantselei.ee/en/supporting-government/top-executives-civil-service/competency-framework.

Fundação Dom Cabral (2018), "Mapas das competências gerenciais", unpublished.

Instituto República (2018), "Relatório da 3ª Conferencia Anual do Instituto República '"Serviço Público: Desafios no Brasil'"", unpublished.

OECD (2019a), The Innovation System of the Public Service of Brazil: An exploration of its past, present and future journey, OECD Publishing, Paris.

OECD (2019b), Recommendation of the Council on Public Service Leadership and Capability, OECD, Paris, https://www.oecd.org/gov/pem/recommendation-on-public-service-leadership-and-capability.htm.

OECD (2017), "Core skills for public sector innovation: A beta model", OECD, Paris.

OECD (2016), "Strategic Human Resources Management Survey", OECD, Paris.

OECD IdeaFactory (2015), "Shaping our future leaders", https://www.oecd.org/forum/about/OECD-2015-IdeaFactory-Shaping-Our-Future-Leaders.pdf.

Treviño, L.K., L.P. Hartman and M. Brown (2000), "Moral person and moral manager: How executives develop a reputation for ethical leadership", California Management Review, Vol. 42/4, pp. 128-142, http://dx.doi.org/10.2307/41166057.

Van Wart, M. (2011), Dynamics of Leadership in Public Service: Theory and Practice, 2nd ed., M.E. Sharpe, Armonk, NY.

Wilson, R. (2013), Anti-Hero: The Hidden Revolution in Leadership and Change, OSCA Agency ltd.

4. Developing the supply of innovation leadership in Brazil's federal administration

This chapter looks at how the supply of innovation skills can be further developed in the pool of current and potential leaders in Brazil's federal administration. More specifically, it looks at the emergence of competency-based training across the federal administration, at the efforts to improve the administration's knowledge about existing skills and subsequent gaps, and about the National School of Public Administration's role in developing leadership skills and competencies. The second part of the chapter identifies some levers to improve the learning culture across the administration, such as the development of networks and partnerships and innovative ways of developing skills.

The statistical data for Israel are supplied by and under the responsibility of the relevant Israeli authorities. The use of such data by the OECD is without prejudice to the status of the Golan Heights, East Jerusalem and Israeli settlements in the West Bank under the terms of international law.

"Supply and demand" is one of the foundational tenets of economics with the goal to seek equilibrium to produce healthy and sustainable economies. The same concept can be applied to leadership competencies such as those discussed in Chapter 3. There needs to be a supply of people with the right competencies ready to take up leadership positions in the government. This suggests the need to provide learning and development opportunities to leaders and to the potential pool of leaders, whether inside the civil service or beyond. However, this supply also has to be matched with a commensurate demand for these skills from those who take appointment decisions. Balancing supply and demand of leadership skills is at the core of senior civil service (SCS) systems. Without this balance, a country is unlikely to have an effective and sustainable leadership system and risks overinvesting in certain areas while not seeing the expected returns.

Much of the interventions so far established in Brazil focus on the "supply" side of skills and competencies – development opportunities for current and future senior leaders. This chapter looks at how the supply of innovation skills can be further developed in the pool of current and potential leaders. More specifically, it will look at the emergence of competency-based training across the federal administration, at the efforts to improve the administration's knowledge about existing skills and subsequent gaps, and about the National School of Public Administration's (Escola nacional de administração pública, ENAP) role in the skills and competencies development landscape. The second part of the chapter identifies some levers to improve the learning culture across the administration, such as the development of networks and partnerships and innovative ways of developing skills.

Skills and competencies in Brazil's federal administration: An overview

In Brazil's civil service, formal training (in particular academic education) tends to be used as an indicator of skill and capability, including for senior leaders. Academic training in a relevant field is usually one of the few criteria to assess candidates' suitability to access the positions in the civil service. The 2019 decree[1] on the "Criteria, Profile and Procedures to Appoint DAS and FCPEs" underlines once more that any appointment (Senior Direction and Counselling Group [Grupo Direção e Assessoramento Superiores, DAS] or "commissioned functions" [funções comissionadas do poder executivo, FCPE]) in the federal administration should be primarily based on a good reputation, relevant professional experience and academic qualifications.

The importance of academic degrees in the federal administration overall has been increasing over the past 20 years. Between 2000 and 2018, the number of federal civil servants with an academic degree[2] increased from 49% to 75% (ENAP, 2018). Among the OECD countries that collect data on the level of civil servants' education, in 2015 in Chile 39% of employees in the central administration held an academic degree,[3] 61% in Australia and Estonia, 62% in Sweden, and 82% in Israel.[4] The strong increase in the academic qualifications of Brazilian civil servants is a consequence of the retirement of civil servants without or with less academic qualifications, but also of an increase of people's qualifications in the overall job market (ENAP, 2018).

After entering the federal administration, leaders and civil servants continue to have access to training opportunities. However, without information about the existing skills and competencies within the system, it is challenging for the federal administration to develop a systematic approach to development.

In this context, training decisions tend to be driven by individuals' motivations and interest. Without individual or organisational planning, training does not always align with someone's relevant responsibilities nor with organisational needs. As training is self-driven and bespoke, it can lead to the exploration of new skills and competencies that generate innovative ideas. Conversely, it can also create an environment in which it is hard to practice and evolve these skills and competencies outside of the classroom and can cause a misalignment with the true needs of the individual, organisation and system. Even when training involves bringing workplace issues into the classroom to create a strong link between work and the training, it is still difficult to replicate workplace conditions such as coalition building, political will and convincing co-workers that may be against the idea.

It is also challenging to address skills gaps. For example, the innovation skills survey conducted for this report (see Chapter 2) highlights that a vast majority of respondents from the federal administration want to improve their skills in at least one of the six areas assessed by the survey[5] (see Figure 1.4 in Chapter 1). Almost 99% of senior civil servants and around 95% of the other categories surveyed responded "Yes" to the question "Do you want to improve your skills in the above-mentioned areas?".

Despite the overall interest for developing one's own skills for innovation, when questioned about the existing opportunities to improve those skills, responses suggest that there is still space to either increase those opportunities, or to improve communication about existing opportunities in the federal government (Figure 4.1). Only 52% of senior civil servants who want to improve their skills consider that they have opportunities to do so. This percentage decreases to 37% for other civil servants. The percentage of respondents who do not know whether there are opportunities available is equivalent in both groups (11% and 12%).

Figure 4.1. Do civil servants who want to improve their innovation skills have the opportunity to do so?

Perception of surveyed employees in the federal administration

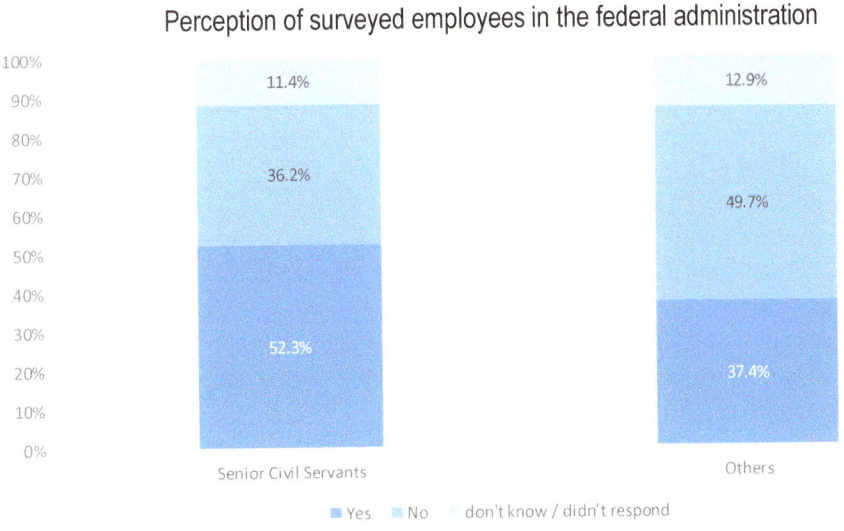

Note: "Senior civil servants" refers to DAS 4-6 and FCPE 4. "Other" refers to DAS and FCPE 1-3 and other civil servants who do not occupy DAS nor FCPE positions.
Source: OECD (2018b), "Survey on Innovation Skills: Organisational Readiness Assessment" (Habilidades de Inovação: Avaliação de Prontidão Organizacional), unpublished.

Identifying and mapping current leadership competencies

Supply-side interventions first require a competency mapping to identify the existing supply. Competency mapping ensures that the skills and competencies are readily identified and available when there is demand. It also helps to better align development initiatives to ensure they are addressing real gaps.

To start addressing this challenge, the former Ministry of Planning, in partnership with ENAP and others, has developed a data bank that has the potential to serve this purpose. This type of initiative has already been used in some of the Brazilian federal administration organisations that carry out selective procedures for appointed positions, like the Bank of Brazil. These internal data banks include information about professional competencies of civil servants who can potentially be qualified for appointed positions (Camões and Balué, 2015) and score potential candidates according to their experience and training. This could be a way to pre-qualify potential civil servant candidates for certain positions. The current database - Sigepe Talent Bank - can potentially start cross-referencing the existing civil service databases to compile more variables, such as skills developed outside work.

Box 4.1. The Sigepe Talent Bank in the Brazilian federal administration

The Sigepe Talent Bank is a platform serving as a skills database for public servants. Public servants can upload their curriculum vitae into the system. The skills information is accessible to any public servant, allowing for a greater understanding of the skills and competencies within teams, organisations and the government as well as more targeted recruiting and hiring based on knowledge, expertise and experience.

This platform was created following a partnership between the Ministry of Economy and the National Council for Scientific and Technological Development (CNPq). The CNPq is responsible for the Lattes Platform, which is a single information system for curricula vitae, and widely used amongst academics and researchers in Brazil.

As more civil servants (and possibly non civil servants in the future) put their data into the system, the higher the potential for better analysis of careers, skills and experiences, to help the federal administration make better training programmes, improve hiring decisions and facilitate the recruitment of qualified candidates.

Source: Interviews, Governo federal (2019), Portal do Servidor, https://www.servidor.gov.br/servicos/faq/banco-de-talentos-perguntas-frequentes

---

By becoming an online repository of civil servants' skills, competencies and experiences, the Talent Bank initiative could help to begin systematising the leadership competency supply which currently exists within the civil service, to ensure that those looking for talent are able to reach beyond their own networks to find it. This may be an important step towards breaking down the reliance on personal networking which currently appears to dominate selection and appointment processes. At the same time, if the database remains exclusive to civil servants, it may reduce the visibility for people who are not civil servants but whose skills could be relevant for DAS positions.

Some OECD countries have been testing similar approaches. The Talent Cloud is one of the most ambitious projects of the government of Canada: this programme aims to become a validated, searchable repository of cross-sector talent (Box 4.2).

Box 4.2. Free Agents and GC Talent Cloud – Canada

The government of Canada proposed to restructure government workforces to meet the changing needs of citizens in complex environments. In this context, Natural Resources Canada set out to test a new form of workforce planning – the GC Talent Cloud. The central idea was that the GC Talent Cloud would become a new digital platform of pre-qualified talent with a competency validation process and easy searchability. Free Agents was one of its earliest pilots to test the feasibility (including market viability, efficiency savings, psychological stress on workers in the gig economy, competency modelling and screening design) of a new type of workforce.

The objectives of the pilot were threefold:

1. demonstrate the benefits of the cloud-based free agency model for human resources
2. support, develop and retain talented public servants
3. increase the capacity of the public service to innovate and solve problems.

As many different types of work could benefit from the model, Natural Resources Canada's Innovation Hub chose to forego the choice of a specific background or skill set for Free Agents. Instead, the Innovation Hub developed a set of attributes and behaviours that the public service innovation community considered valuable for innovation and problem solving in their organisations. These attributes formed the basis for the pilot's screening process.

Candidates who successfully demonstrate these core attributes are offered lateral deployments to positions in a special unit of the Natural Resources Canada Innovation Hub. Because of the lateral deployment model, there is flexibility in the selection process and assessment methodology. Deployments do not need to have clear priorities or undergo a competitive process for appointment.

The Free Agent pilot tracks performance, project outcomes, costs, risks and benefits in order to make broad, data-driven recommendations about the long-term viability of the potential full-scale GC Talent Cloud model. Work is underway to develop a profile of skills and competencies useful for innovation in the public service. Once developed, this profile will provide the framework for Free Agents to pursue training and learning opportunities.

Source: OECD (2018a), Embracing Innovation in Government: Global Trends 2018, https://www.oecd.org/gov/innovative-government/embracing-innovation-in-government-2018.pdf

In parallel, the former Ministry of Planning has conducted a census of civil servants from the specialist in public policy and government management career. In partnership with the National School of Public Administration, in the second half of 2018 the Secretary of Management undertook a Demographic and Professional Trajectory Census of specialists in public policy and government management, in order to better understand who government managers are, where they are and what results they have helped to achieve in the federal public administration. This census is expected to provide better knowledge of the civil servants from this career, their career paths, experience and skills.

The emergence of competency-based leadership training in Brazil

More information about the available skills should help Brazil move forward with the competency-based approach designed back in 2006. Competency-based management (gestão por competências) was introduced in 2006[6] to help plan, monitor and assess capacity-building activities. Its focus was on identifying the knowledge, skills and attitudes needed to perform civil service functions.[7] While this has yet to formalise into a national competency framework, it has served as a driver for reorienting and strengthening training opportunities and individual development.

The gradual emergence of competency frameworks in different institutions across the Brazilian federal administration and beyond is a strong indicator that organisations are open to taking a more structured approach to leadership development. Competency models have become foundational in leadership training. Various institutions in the Brazilian federal public administration, including the former Ministry of Planning, ENAP, the Court of Accounts and the Brazilian Development Bank, have developed their own frameworks to anchor their leadership development programmes (see Chapter 2). All of these programmes were created with the recognition that existing opportunities for leadership development were insufficient.

In parallel, Brazil's Staff Development Policy and Guidelines[8] regulate professional development through annual training plans for public organisations. Until 2010[9] this policy was steered by a committee which included the Secretary of Management (SEGES), the Secretariat of Personnel Management (SEGEP) and ENAP. While this policy acknowledged the importance of professional development, it never lived up to initial expectations. The evolution of the political context since its approval led to regular changes in priorities and operational objectives, as well as to the difficult task of co-ordinating multiple decision makers with conflicting priorities (Camões and Meneses, 2016).

The current legal basis to train people for DAS and FCPE positions[10] is the same decree that introduced competency-based training in the federal administration. This decree also gives ENAP the responsibility to co-ordinate and oversee the management of training programmes for civil servants by schools of government of the federal administration, municipalities and foundations.

ENAP: A core institution for developing innovation skills

ENAP has been critical to the development of a competency-based approach by focusing on skills development through Masters, leadership development, senior executive programmes as well as specialised and general skills training. ENAP has gradually assumed the role of an informal "hub" or adviser for many leadership programmes. Although ENAP does not have the authority or ability to create a singular leadership curriculum that organisations use to develop leaders, the school's presence in the formation of many of the existing programmes at least promotes a general coherence in the competency models and convergence in ideas and theories.

ENAP has also gradually become a hub for innovation skills development in the last few years. As of 2016 ENAP became a scientific, technological and innovation institution (instituição científica, tecnológica e de inovação), responsible for research and service development relevant to improve the efficiency and the quality of public services. The 2019 decree[11] reinforces ENAP's role in this field by centralising in ENAP the elaboration and execution of staff development programmes related to public sector innovation for improving the efficiency and quality of the services provided to citizens.

The development of public sector innovation within public administration schools is also common in some OECD countries. In France, ENAP's French homologue (École nationale d'administration) is one of the founding members of the Chaire Innovation Publique, one of the first cross-cutting attempts to transform the future of working in the public sector through innovation. In Spain, a 2018 amendment created a Department of Public Sector Innovation in the Institute of Public Administration (INAP), and INAP is gradually becoming a key player in the process of transforming the public administration. To support the emergence of a culture of skills for transformation and innovation, INAP is investing in projects to develop a competency-based approach across the administration (Box 4.3).

Box 4.3. Investing in skills for public sector innovation in Spain

The Spanish Institute for Public Sector Innovation (INAP) is an autonomous body responsible for the training of civil servants at all levels. INAP introduced a Department of Public Sector Innovation in 2018 to support the institute's mission to transform the Spanish public administration and better address the needs of citizens.

One of the key areas of concern for the new department is new skills for the civil service, linked to the work that the institute is carrying out on the Sustainable Development Goals Agenda, digitalisation, social change and new realities. In this framework, the department is working to improve innovation skills in four areas:

1. establishment of a common methodology for the detection of training needs
2. preparation of skills models for different professional profiles
3. promotion of an approval and certification model for qualifications valid for all administrations (national and regional)
4. development and application of evaluation methodologies acquired formally and informally.

The department's work aims to contribute to INAP's ambition to become increasingly democratic, inclusive, diverse, sustainable, representative and aligned with the society it serves. To serve this

---

purpose, focus is given to improving its selection processes and attracting valuable and diverse (highly skilled) talent, learning values, competencies and skills of public servants, and reflection and research on the challenges facing the state and its public administrations within a framework of partnerships.

Source: INAP's presentation in the 6th Annual Meeting of the OECD Global Network of Schools of Government, Helsinki, September 2018.

From bespoke to systemic: Moving away from classroom training to creating a learning culture for innovation in the senior civil service

To shift a learning culture from sporadic to systemic also requires a review of the proper drivers that would encourage and push current and future leaders to obtain these skills and competencies. From the supply side, there needs to be a multi-method approach that allows people to learn in different and new ways, both in specialised programmes and also every day on the job. However, to truly have a systemic approach to a learning culture, there must be a demand for the skills that public leaders need. The 2019 OECD Recommendation of the Council on Public Service Leadership and Capability highlights many of these elements (Box 4.4).

Box 4.4. Learning culture in the OECD Recommendation of the Council on Public Service Leadership and Capability

The OECD's Recommendation of the Council on Public Service Leadership and Capability recognises the fundamental need to develop a learning culture in public sector institutions. Under the Recommendation's second pillar on "investing in public service capability in order to develop an effective and trusted public service", OECD countries emphasise the contribution learning makes to this, by:

Developing the necessary skills and competencies by creating a learning culture and environment in the public service, in particular through:

1. identifying employee development as a core management task of every public manager and encouraging the use of employees' full skill sets
2. encouraging and incentivising employees to proactively engage in continuous self-development and learning, and providing them with quality opportunities to do so and
3. valuing different learning approaches and contexts, linked to the type of skill set and ambition or capacity of the learner.

Source: OECD, Recommendation of the Council on Public Service Leadership and Capability, OECD/LEGAL/0445

Developing a skill or competency can be a targeted and finite activity, and may be a first step towards developing a learning culture. However, a culture of continuous learning requires a consistent focus on creating environments where employees are encouraged and supported to learn and develop their skills and competencies – both existing and new. Most skills and competencies are not binary where one either "has" or "does not have" it. Instead, it is often evolutionary where it takes time, practice and experience to master. Traditionally skills and competencies have been taught in a controlled environment, such as a classroom or lab, and then participants are expected to start using these out in the real world. More recently, experiential training has become popular – learning through hands-on experience, by doing the work with appropriate guidance and support.

One of the challenges of experiential learning, particularly for leaders, is that it requires a high level of self-awareness and space for reflection. This goes against the traditional notion that leaders are the smartest and most experienced in the organisation. However, the idea that everybody is a novice and able to learn from experience is a fundamental tenet of innovation, since, by definition, participants are trying something new. This is aligned with the anti-hero approach to modern public leadership discussed in Chapter 3. The Dutch government has developed a vision for public sector leadership which focuses on three core competencies: integrity, collaboration and reflection (Box 4.5). Reflection recognises the need for leaders to take the time from their hectic daily schedules to reflect on their craft and learn from experience.

Box 4.5. Dutch vision of public sector leadership

The Dutch vision of public sector leadership recognises that there is not one single ideal type of leader; rather there are qualities every public leader should show:

1. Integrity: The public leader works sincerely and consciously in the public interest, addresses the social issues and demonstrates this in his/her daily actions.

2. Co-operation: The public leader puts shared leadership into practice, is focused on the broader context and not exclusively his/her "own" domain, actively seeks collaboration and co-creation, and is able to understand various perspectives.

3. Reflection: The public leader has self-awareness and organises reflection in the field based on knowledge and practice, asks the right questions, and accordingly determines the course and position.

Figure 4.2. Vision of Public Sector Leadership in the Netherlands

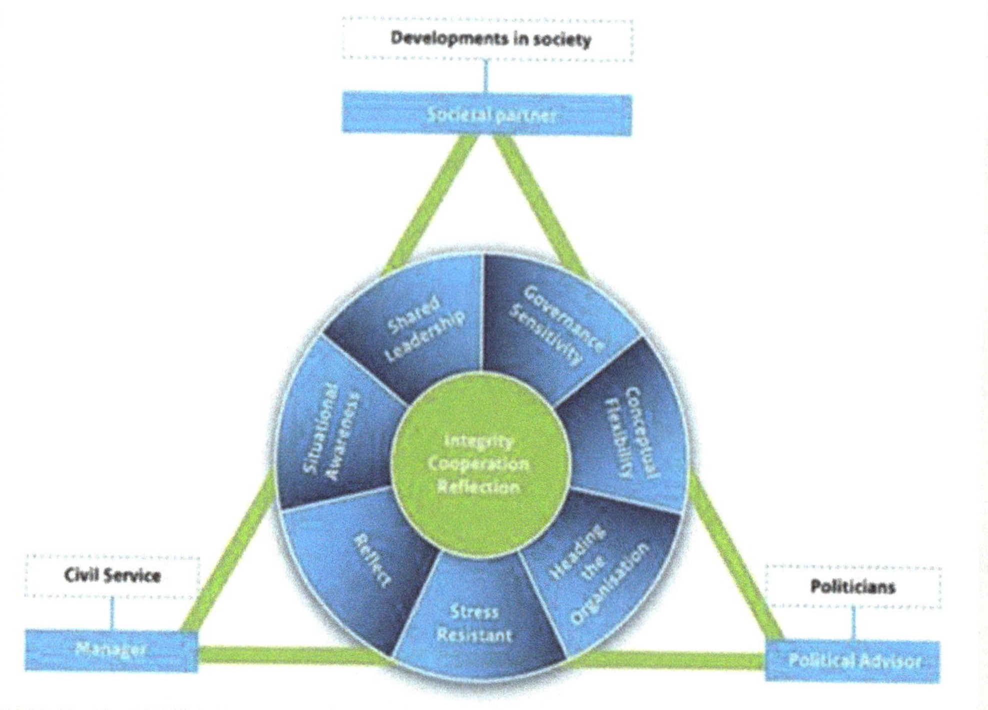

Source: Information provided to the OECD by the Office for the Senior Civil Service, Netherlands.

Competency models such as those discussed in Chapter 3 serve as a guide to help guide training programmes for leaders and potential leaders, but as the skills needed evolve and new skills emerge, competency models alone do not create a learning culture. Additionally, during a time of potential fiscal austerity, training dollars become scarce, which limits traditional training opportunities for leaders and employees. In the aftermath of the 2008 financial crisis, most OECD countries reported that their training policies in central public administration were affected. While nineteen countries implemented measures to raise the efficiency of training, 16 reduced training budgets; and ten reduced the number of training days (OECD, 2016).

Because each person learns differently, there is no single solution to this issue. Instead, multiple approaches are required. There need to be solutions that incorporate classroom learning, experiential learning and peer learning. Additionally, employee development needs to be something that every people manager commits to. This means ensuring that managers are given the skills, competencies and tools to manage their teams in ways that integrate learning into their everyday work. This can be as simple as developing regular opportunities for their employees to learn from each others' ongoing projects, and/or assigning tasks in ways that expand employees' capabilities. In Ireland, a core pillar of the recent Civil Service People Strategy is to ensure that every manager is a people developer. In Finland, leaders meet once a month around various leadership topics. Leaders self-select which topic they want to address and it is relatively self-organised.

Box 4.6. Developing a learning culture through Ireland's Civil Service People Strategy

The third pillar of Ireland's Civil Service People Strategy 2017-2020 is entitled "Build, Support and Value Managers as People Developers" and sets an outcome target of, "the civil service has great people managers enabling civil servants to perform to the highest levels and fulfil their potential."

The actions laid out in this part of the people strategy commits the civil service to "foster a stronger culture of good people management by re-emphasising the people management role for all managers, so that they understand what is expected of them. Organisational HR units (OHRs) will support people managers by ensuring that they have access to effective tools, supports, professional HR advice and expertise, so that managers can further develop their capacity and confidence to deal with all people management issues. OHRs will be supported by a Central HR Advisory Service so that they can build the supports and services necessary to provide services to people managers. Managers at all levels will develop a stronger collaborative management culture by recognising and modelling good people management practices enabling the creation of a high performing work environment with the right conditions for dealing effectively with underperformance."

Source: Civil Service HR Division (2017), "People Strategy for the Civil Service 2017-2020", https://hr.per.gov.ie/wp-content/uploads/People-Strategy-for-the-Civil-Service-2017-2020.pdf.

Transforming executive innovation training

New forms of executive innovation training are emerging in Brazil and in many OECD countries. These trainings, often conducted by innovation labs in the civil service, are focused on helping leaders understand how to lead innovative projects and provide the support necessary for innovation to thrive. The Government Digital Services in the United Kingdom has developed an Agile for Leadership class, the Canadian government is looking at something similar regarding digital competencies, and Chile and Colombia actively engage senior leaders when their teams are engaged in innovation challenges through the country's innovation labs. All of these initiatives allow leadership to gain first-hand experience in how innovation happens to better understand how they can support it.

Canada's Digital Academy was launched in 2018 with the purpose of "placing the public service at the forefront of the digital age and to making its services more secure, faster and easier for all users". The academy is hosted at the Canada School of Public Service, and its curriculum will support all levels of public servants, including senior civil servants (Box 4.7).

Box 4.7. Canada's Digital Executive Leadership Program

The Digital Executive Leadership Program, launched by the Canadian Institute on Governance, is part of the government of Canada's Digital Academy initiative. The five-day course aims to provide public sector executives at all levels of government (federal, provincial, municipal) with the digital literacy and leadership skills they need to be effective decision makers in the rapidly changing policy and service delivery landscape.

The focus for the programme is centered on three core areas and how they are changing the landscape for governance, service delivery and policy development in the public sector: design thinking, digital technologies and data. The course provides participants with a basic grounding in key concepts from each of these three disciplines, and a practical understanding of how they can be applied to the business of government. In addition, the programme also provides participants with an understanding of the big strategic drivers of the digital era, and considerations for building and managing modern, digitally savvy teams in the public sector.

Source: Institute on Governance (2018), Digital Executive Leadership Program, in https://iog.ca/leadership-learning/digital/ (accessed 26 September 2019).

In Estonia, the Top Civil Service Excellence Centre is responsible for the development of Estonia's senior civil servants. It has developed a training programme that focuses on experiential learning, applying modern problem-solving techniques, and even brain science to help leaders better understand themselves, build innovation skills and conduct activities on site where "seeing is believing". This programme has gained such popularity that the governments of Finland, the Netherlands and the United Kingdom requested their leaders participate.

ENAP's Training Programme for Senior Executives (Programa de Capacitação para Altos Executivos) has become a reference in the field of executive leadership training in Brazil's public sector, and includes an important component on innovation. Created as a pilot project at the end of 2015, this programme was one of the most recent initiatives to map and develop the skills and competencies required to professionalise politically appointed public leaders. ENAP's training is not mandatory, so the strategy is about creating a diversified offer in terms of themes and formats to nudge leaders into self-selecting for training.

By targeting training at appointed SCS positions, ENAP is also building bridges between the political and the administrative spheres. Especially within Brazil's system where the political-administrative interface is blurred, transforming the public sector in a sustainable way requires preparing leadership to face technical and political challenges, regardless of whether they are appointed from the civil service or from other sectors. To address this, ENAP's approach is designed around real-life leadership challenges. This programme also offers different learning modalities to build these bridges, ranging from international training cycles, conferences and individual coaching to more informal events such as thematic dinners for senior executives and gatherings of the programme's alumni.

The complexity of leadership and its challenges also means that developing leaders is more than a repetitive exercise; it is an iterative process. ENAP's different training programmes are dynamic and grounded in partnerships with prestigious training institutions worldwide, namely the John F. Kennedy School of Government, Harvard University and the French School of Public Administration. One of the most recent editions (August 2018) focused on "Leadership and Innovation in a Context of Change". During the course, participants worked on an ongoing challenge while developing skills and competencies related to adaptive leadership, technology management or innovation in public policies.

ENAP's iterative approach to the Training Programme for Senior Executives involved testing different practice-oriented methodologies leading to a wide variety of complementary learning paths (Box 4.8). The programme's success following ENAP's restructuring in 2016 created the opportunity to strengthen

ENAP's mission to "plan, direct, co ordinate, guide and evaluate the training offer for senior executives". ENAP's Leadership Development Programme, a project-oriented course focused on developing business acumen in particular areas and innovative skills, combines online preparation and discussion with classroom training, and is targeted at managerial positions across the federal government.

Box 4.8. ENAP – School of Government

Improving the skills of public servants

Created in 1986, the National School of Public Administration (ENAP) is a public foundation whose purpose is to promote, design and execute human resources training programmes for the federal administration.

It has also collaborated with outside organisations to bring advanced thinking around public sector leadership. For instance, ENAP partnered with Harvard University for a leadership programme with DAS* 5 and 6, as well as people in positions of "special nature", such as ministers and vice -ministers. Bringing in outside partners helps to ensure content is current, timely and allows for multiple perspectives from inside and outside the current system.

ENAP was one of the first organisations in Brazil to create innovation training and competency models for training programmes. Starting in 1996, ENAP and the former Ministry of Planning, Development and Management also created the Innovation Award to celebrate innovators and their projects to improve services to the population.

In addition, the OECD observed ENAP's role in the evolution and promotion of public sector innovation in Brazil. ENAP is serving as an informal "hub" for innovation programmes and training, working with various public sector organisations and civil society to promote, enhance and spread best practices of innovation training.

Leadership training

ENAP's mandate on leadership training evolved with Decree No. 8.902/2016, which stressed that one of ENAP's missions was to support and promote training programmes for people in leadership positions (DAS and "commissioned functions" [FCPE]). As part of its new mission, ENAP strengthened its partnerships with international leadership training institutions to develop and deliver short-term courses in areas related to innovative leadership in public organisations (Programa de Capacitação para Altos Executivos). Recent training offer for senior executives includes experiential and problem focused training programmes, in-company consultancy, and informal events for senior managers.

Note : * Senior Direction and Counselling Group.
Source: https://www.enap.gov.br.

There are also cases across the federal administration where civil servants were encouraged to attend leadership training programmes. A programme in the former Ministry of Planning established that civil servants could take training leave for priority fields for the ministry such as leadership, economics or public administration. Civil servants applied to the programme through a selection process, then were eligible to attend long-term courses, including Master and PhD degrees. The increase in the qualification of the ministry's staff led in practice to an increase in the qualification of the people later appointed for leadership positions.

Investing in leadership development for innovation raises a challenge about ensuring the quality and impact of the training provided. In this context, it could be relevant to develop some sort of certification mechanism, such as, for example, France's "School of Management and Human Resources" label, which consists in the certification, by a committee of independent experts, of training programmes which are either interministerial or relevant for more than one ministry. Despite the benefits of certification, attention should be paid to avoid creating overburdening processes.

To strengthen coherence around public sector innovation, France's Interministerial Directorate for Public Transformation (Direction Interministérielle pour la Transformation Publique), under the Prime Minister's Office, has created a "Public Transformation Campus". The campus provides team training on project management, user centricity, digital, innovative approaches and managerial transformation. It also brought together respected actors in the field of innovation training in France. This includes, for example, the National School of Administration (École Nationale d'Administration), the Institute for Public Management and Economic Development (Institut de la Gestion Publique et du Développement Économique), or the National Centre for Territorial Civil Service (Centre National de la Fonction Publique Territoriale). The campus aims to develop synergies among existing training programmes and promotes the training delivered by its partners.

Reinventing skills development through innovation labs

ENAP's innovation lab, GNova, uses design-thinking methodologies to help public institutions address their challenges. GNova's approach is an interesting way to link experiential learning with classroom training by supporting bottom-up innovation processes, also tested in other countries. Teams from GNova partner with the civil servants from the client organisation to co-create and experiment solutions and prototypes, for example to improve the delivery of services to citizens.

In Chile, the Laboratorio de Gobierno developed a programme called Experimenta to develop innovation skills in a selected group of public employees through a learning-by-doing approach. This "learning-by-doing" approach whereby innovation labs partner with other public sector organisations to collaborate, co-create and design has become a popular and effective way to build innovation capacity and experience in organisations.

Investing in collaborative partnerships beyond the public sector

ENAP and other public sector organisations are not the only actors interested in improving the competencies of public leaders to steer public sector innovation in Brazil. Civil society is playing a key role in advancing innovation skills in the public sector. For example, the "Support Programme for the Development of Public Leadership" has emerged to help build public leaders' capacity, including elected officials, engaged in changing Brazil based on the principles of integrity, democracy and sustainability. The programme is the result of a partnership between the "Political Action Network for Sustainability (Rede de Ação Política pela Sustentabilidade) and the Lemann Foundation. The content is developed by the two partner institutions and includes training on themes such as health, public safety and climate change. The second edition (2018) was open to 20 leaders throughout Brazil. Other examples include the Dom Cabral Foundation, which is working with ENAP, the Ministry of Economy (previously Ministry of Planning) and others on leadership training and development based on various leadership competency models; and the Getúlio Vargas Foundation has also created leadership programmes aimed at the public sector. These organisations are playing an important role to help develop a more mature understanding of the competencies needed for public sector leaders in Brazil and to bridge the gap between the public sector and civil society, the private sector, and academia.

Collaborative partnerships between the public sector and external stakeholders can help advance public leadership for innovation. Such partnerships can create access to a wider body of knowledge, perspective and technology, and help generate a better understanding of problems, policy issues, and define and test potential solutions (see, for example, OECD 2017b). In the field of leadership skills and competencies for innovation, the launch of the Public Innovation Chair (Chaire Innovation Publique, CIP) in France provides a good example of this type of collaborative partnerships. The CIP's approach focuses on bringing in different stakeholders to prepare current and future senior civil servants to innovate through design, digital technology and behavioural insights.

Box 4.9. Public Innovation Chair: A new approach to public policies in France

The Public Innovation Chair (CIP) aims to be a new space to co-create the 21st century administration through a multidisciplinary and iterative approach to policy making and public service delivery. The CIP looks at how public sector innovation (often based on concepts from design, behavioural economics or digital transformation) challenges the traditional ways of working and affects the way people and resources are managed, and how decisions are taken. This means looking at the impact of digital transformation (including digital governance or use of data); user-centered design (starting from the experience of users, civil servants and citizens); and new ways of working (including labs, open innovation, agile innovation, start-up mode).

The Public Innovation Chair works to mainstream innovation, including among public sector leaders. By helping senior civil servants understand new ways of working in government, they contribute to government innovation and are better placed to incentivise innovation in the organisations they lead. In this context, the CIP aims to:

1. experiment by supporting innovative field projects
2. advance research and analysis to understand how public administration is changing at national and territorial level
3. monitor progress and share knowledge on innovation
4. learn innovation through initial or continuous training.

The CIP is not a traditional academic chair and none of its core partner institutions have a permanent body of professors. While this characteristic means that the CIP's leadership may not be clear in the public sector landscape, it also creates space for more flexibility and scaling up.

Source: ENA/ENSCI (2017), Presentation of the Public Innovation Chair.

Using networks to support innovators

Interest in public sector innovation has been growing throughout the Brazilian federal administration. The public innovation awards were established in 1996 to reward new ways of working in the public sector. In 2016, the then Ministry of Planning and ENAP organised the first Innovation Week and ENAP hosted the first innovation lab (GNova). In parallel, public sector innovation became a growing field of research among Brazilian academics and practitioners. Some of the first reflections and analysis of the Brazilian experience helped map trends, success stories, opportunities and barriers for innovation (see, for example, ENAP/IPEA [2017]).

Innovation remained a relatively isolated activity in the federal administration landscape. While awards and events celebrated innovation across the public sector, initiatives and teams remain the exceptional way of working in the administration. The lack of a clear mandate to innovate possibly reinforced the perception of risk associated with innovation; most innovations are very context-specific, which made them hard to scale up or to replicate in different contexts (ENAP/IPEA, 2017).

Despite little systematisation of innovation across the administration, the success stories helped support an emerging innovation-oriented organisational culture. Awards and events give visibility to initiatives and help people learn from each other's experience (OECD, 2015), which can help motivate civil servants. Awards are widely used across OECD countries to recognise successful public sector innovation in different areas of the civil service. In the United States, the Presidential Rank Awards Programme recognises a select group of career members of the Senior Executive Service for exceptional performance. In Chile, the Funciona! recognises teams of civil servants who have created innovative initiatives in their institutions, with an effect on internal efficiency and/or in the quality of services provided to citizens (OECD, 2017a).

Besides giving visibility to innovations, events and awards can also help to build a community of practice around innovation. Innovators are change agents and, as such, they often struggle to get support within their own organisations. Facilitating communication between innovators, who often face similar challenges, can help them support each other, strengthen their motivation and capacity for action, and even help scale up innovations (OECD, 2017). This type of informal, self-driven network is a common form of innovators networks in OECD countries. In Finland, for example, the Change Makers network is a loosely organised and self-managed team of experts from different ministries, with different backgrounds, education and expertise. What is shared among the participants is the need and the will to build up a working culture based on a "whole government" mindset and "crossing the silos" ways of working.

Institutional support to networks of innovators is also an important element to strengthen the visibility and impact of public sector innovation. Formalising innovation networks can help give consistency to different networks, creating a coherent vision of innovation, and consolidating the impact of the network on the public innovation landscape. The gradual launch since 2015 of InovaGov, the Federal Network of Innovation in the Public Sector (Rede Federal de Inovação no Setor Público) responds to that need to formalise networks of innovators. In the Brazilian federal administration context, formalising a network for innovation may also give some legitimacy to time spent on innovation (ENAP/IPEA, 2017). Developed by the Department of Public Management Modernization (Departamento de Modernização em Gestão Pública, Inova) of the former Ministry of Planning, the InovaGov was supported by strong institutional actors such as the Court of Accounts (Tribunal de Contas da União) and the Council of Federal Justice (Conselho de Justiça Federal). InovaGov has grown to become a space where different sectors interact. It creates value by opening the discussions outside the public sector to include businesses, academia and non-governmental organisations.

Networks of innovators are also common across most OECD countries. Similarly to InovaGov, the most common purpose of innovators networks in OECD countries is to help members share their experience, like Portugal's Common Knowledge Network RCC, which is a collaborative platform to promote the sharing of practices and information about modernisation, innovation and simplification of public administration.

The development of InovaGov raises questions about the role of Inova and of the Ministry of Economy in building the supply of skills for innovation. In many OECD countries, innovators networks build the capacities of members through training provide support to develop specific projects or guidance to public institutions (OECD, 2017). In Chile, the Network of Public Innovators, created in 2015, aims at being a movement of diverse actors motivated by the search for tools, experiences and approaches that facilitate the development of innovations to improve public services for their users. The network employs a threefold strategy that includes collective learning, making public innovation visible and connecting motivations to innovate (OECD, 2017).

While capacity building is not at the core of InovaGov, the network's missions naturally include some capacity building about innovation tools and practices. Co-ordinating with other training providers, in particular ENAP, is fundamental to develop a shared vision and approach to innovation for Brazil's federal administration. Having a coherent approach to skills and competencies development can help identify common challenges and needs, in a context of heterogeneity of skills and competencies needs and a myriad of public sector careers that hamper career mobility. As described above, coherence is particularly important when it comes to leaders' skills and competencies to support innovation.

ENAP is also exploring the potential of formal and informal networks to improve the impact of its leadership programmes. Informal thematic discussions and dinners such as those organised by ENAP, between senior civil servants from different administrations and experts, have the potential to help leaders exchange experiences and discuss challenges, which often help identify shared concerns or commonalities. OECD research indicates that while most OECD countries provide institutional support for innovators networks, informal and self-driven public sector innovation networks are even more common across the OECD (2016a).

Another of ENAP's major initiative is the Alumni Network of the Senior Executive Training. Regular events for alumni allow them to strengthen personal and professional networks and build additional value from continuous training.

Finally, formalising networks should not come at the expense of informal or non-governmental initiatives. Individual motivation is a powerful driver of innovation and appears to have more influence on the outcome of innovation than formal processes (see, for example, ENAP/IPEA [2017]). In fact, in the past years, Brazil's civil society has been increasingly involved in discussions to improve innovation and, more broadly, the quality of the public sector. Various initiatives have emerged from the civil society involving the municipal, state and federal level.

The civil society organisation Vetor Brasil has been helping municipalities and states to recruit public leaders and trainees (see Chapter 5). Since its creation in 2015, the recruitment programmes developed by Vetor have enabled the creation of a network of talented and engaged professionals that support excellence in the public service. Likewise, the civil society organisation Brava works to support innovation and digitalisation across government in order to improve public management. It brings together stakeholders and innovators to support a culture of better public management. Brava's initiatives include working with schools to help students understand policy making and stimulate critical thinking. Brava has also set up an open online platform to inform citizens about public challenges and help identify innovative solutions.

Box 4.10. Vetor Brasil: Networking for public sector impact

Vetor Brasil is a non-profit civil society organisation working to improve the governance of the public sector. Since 2015, Vetor Brasil has collaborated with public institutions to improve human resource management skills in the government, including to develop new strategies to attract, select and develop public sector professionals.

Vetor's programme "Leaders of Public Management" (Programa Líderes de Gestão Pública) is based on partnerships, mainly with local and state level administrations. Vetor's approach includes a skills diagnosis and pre-selection of qualified candidates. After the hiring decision (by the public authority), the selected candidate becomes a member of Vetor's professional network. The network aims to empower and support these leaders throughout their careers in the public sector.

Source: Interviews and Vetor Brasil, in https://vetorbrasil.org/

Recommendations and roadmap

Ensuring there is a proper supply of the skills and competencies for public sector leaders requires an ongoing, systemic approach that needs constant and consistent oversight, nurturing, and long-term planning and flexibility. There will always be a need for adaptation and flexibility of leadership styles and competencies due to the breadth of activities and responsibilities within the public sector. At the same time, a bespoke training model whereby each ministry and institution is individually responsible for ensuring a supply of current and future leaders will only serve to reinforce the fragmentation of the current model in Brazil.

These recommendations therefore focus on activities that shift the learning culture from sporadic to systemic. While every ministry will have a role in the shift, the OECD recognises the importance of ENAP and the Secretariat of Planning and Management in the Ministry of Economy as the main stakeholders to lead the reforms, reinforce and oversee the continuous learning culture in the Brazilian public sector.

For supply-related recommendations, there are two clear areas of focus: create a trusted ecosystem with a unified view of leadership and ensure the training that is offered actually supports and enables this unified view to become a reality. Additionally, the need for constant internal and external communications and feedback is critical for these initiatives. As stated in the OECD's upcoming public sector innovation review of Brazil, the need for clarity and clear signals as to what is expected is critical to many innovative initiatives (OECD, 2019 forthcoming).

Strong learning cultures are dynamic, flexible, constantly experimenting to explore what works, and comprise a variety of diverse activities. Because of this complexity, the recommendations are separated into:

Immediate: Activities that can begin immediately and are logical next steps based on the understanding of the current system.

Second-stage: Activities that represent the logical follow-up to the short-term recommendations. These activities will require some reassessment based on feedback and outcomes of the implementation of the short-term recommendations.

Longer term: Activities that require careful planning, greater investment, more time and a strong systemic foundation. These recommendations will need additional evaluation as changes in complex and dynamic systems are difficult to predict over a long time frame.

Table 4.1. Roadmap for supply-side recommendations

	Immediate recommendations	Second-stage recommendations	Longer term recommendations
Creating a collaborative and unified view of innovative leadership	Serve as a hub and build a trusted network while influencing leadership development (ENAP)	Use the network to develop a more unified innovative leadership competency model	Align the ecosystem of leadership development
Ensuring training is responsive, effective and available	Create greater transparency of training offerings while also expanding experiential training	Conduct a skills analysis based on the newly created competency model	Ensure the training offered is aligned with both the competency model and skills analysis
Communication and feedback			

Immediate recommendations

As discussed earlier in the chapter, ENAP has served as both an informal hub for leadership programmes and an early adopter in recognising innovative competencies, creating new curriculum and experimenting with new training models. Because of its unique position and its mission, ENAP is already well positioned to increase its role in promoting and establishing a stronger learning culture in Brazil's public service today and in the future.

As neither ENAP nor the Secretariat of Planning and Management are likely to be given legal purview over all leadership professional development, both could continue to play a role in the broader system. This means continuing to **encourage training providers to work with networks within and outside the civil service**. These networks have relevant knowledge and experience which could benefit training programmes, strengthen the link between learning and implementation, and help build stronger bonds between leaders and future leaders in various areas.

Additionally, the Secretariat of Planning and Management could also have the responsibility to **make training information easily available** for senior civil servants, civil servants and people working in the federal administration. This could be inspired by what already exists in the "Portal do Servidor," and could consist of an online tool compiling all the information available on training available by topic, tool, date, target group, type of training, price and any other information that might be useful.

Lastly, GNova and ENAP could **further develop experiential training methods** that connect implementation of innovative projects with capacity building, including at the leadership level. GNova's training approach for civil servants is a relatively recent one, and will need further iteration. Once the programme is relatively stable, the focus could shift to capacity, scale and replication for an even greater impact.

Second-stage recommendations

ENAP could use its trusted network and expertise to **create a unified competency model** that can be the foundation of leadership training across the Brazilian ecosystem. This competency model does not need to be built from scratch – ENAP and other organisations should review their own competency models as well as the OECD model from Chapter 3 to firmly establish a leadership competency model that properly emphasises the competencies and skills that Brazil requires of its leaders, especially with innovation skills and mindsets. ENAP should not pursue this alone; it should collaborate with outside organisations, civil society and ministries to co-create an inclusive, shared solution.

The competency framework can also be used to assess **the current skills and talents to establish a baseline** within the public administration, specific organisations or careers. The Secretariat of Planning and Management could partner with ENAP to pilot a competency assessment methodology. This pilot could be across one ministry, or within a single career, with a view to expanding it in a phased approach. The assessment could use information that is already available, such as that from the Talent Bank (see Box 4.14), which could also align with the competency model to standardise its approach to competency identification and assessment.

Lastly, ENAP could **align training with any specific gaps identified based on current available data**. With the Talent Bank and the OECD survey, there are already some data to determine if any adjustments need to be made in the training curriculum to ensure that ENAP is responsive to the current strengths and weaknesses within the public sector.

Longer term recommendations

Major changes in a large and complex system like the public sector will produce unexpected outcomes. Trying to evolve and improve the learning system in Brazil's public sector requires both short-term agility and long-term perspective. Because of this dynamic, the recommendations in this section may continue to evolve and change.

In the longer term it could be useful to **more clearly define the roles of the various actors in the system**. While there does not need to be a single owner of the leadership development system, the lack of defined roles and responsibilities can cause adoption to slow or stall. The role of ENAP and the Secretariat of Planning and Management are both central, but so is the role of the Staff Development Policy Committee and how it engages with the responsibility to recruit, develop and use innovation-related skills. The role of ministries, institutions, careers and outside actors could also be defined. As with any living system, these roles will continue to shift and evolve, but creating an understanding of the roles and responsibilities in the system to track their evolution will be important so as to better integrate activities, reduce overlap and duplication, and address gaps and emerging needs. This may require the establishment of a training council that can serve to co-ordinate the system and update roles and responsibilities as they evolve.

As with any new model for leadership competencies, training providers could conduct a self-assessment to **align training offerings with the new model** to ensure the outcomes of the training will produce the newly defined skills and competencies. Based on ENAP's extensive training, it is likely that much of the training is already fairly aligned, but tweaks may need to be made. Additional adjustment could be considered based on the findings from the public sector competency assessments. For instance, ENAP may invest too heavily, in terms of frequency of classes and curriculum development, in one competency while there are large gaps in a different competency which is going underserved. Again, the Talent Bank – which may need to be tweaked to align with the model – and the OECD survey can serve as a starting point for this analysis.

Regarding roles, ENAP could continue to **develop partnerships with other training providers**. No organisation has the capacity to train the entire public service, and ENAP should continue to look for trusted partners at the local, national and international level to improve innovative leadership. This also includes civil society organisations and networks both inside and outside the civil service.

Communication and feedback

As with any large-scale initiative that impacts the whole of government, communication with clear signals is critical to success. Communication is needed throughout the process and must be done in a way that can elicit feedback. Communication can serve purposes such as:

- sending a clear signal of what is important
- sharing a consistent vision across the ecosystem
- influencing and impacting behaviours
- allowing for feedback more easily.

For instance, the Secretariat of Planning and Management should work with ENAP to increase the understanding of innovation and innovative leadership through a constant and diverse communication plan. Part of this plan could link to specific trainings, but it should also specifically focus on winning the hearts and minds of the public sector with an aspirational vision for current and future leaders. Because of ENAP's role of creating competency frameworks and curriculum as well as its informal role of supporting other public sector leadership programmes within various ministries and institutions, it is in a unique position to directly influence other institutions and ministries in terms of adopting the framework.

Notes

[1] Decree No. 9.727

[2] Degree, post-graduate, Master or PhD

[3] Bachelor, Master or Doctoral degree

[4] Data from 2015, collected through the 2016 OECD survey on the composition of the workforce.

[5] Iteration, data literacy, user centricity, curiosity, storytelling or insurgency

[6] Decree No. 208 of 25 July 2006, Ministry of Planning

[7] Free translation: "ferramenta gerencial que permite planejar, monitorar e avaliar ações de capacitação a partir da identificação dos conhecimentos, das habilidades e das atitudes necessárias ao desempenho das funções dos servidores".

[8] Decree No. 5.707-2006 on the policies and guidelines to staff development in the federal direct, municipal and foundational administration, regulating Law 8.112 of 11 December 1990), available at: www.planalto.gov.br/ccivil_03/_Ato2004-2006/2006/Decreto/D5707.htm (accessed 22 October 2018)

[9] In 2010, the Secretary of Management became part of SEGEP, which also included the Secretariat of Human Resources. A 2016 decree recreated the secretariats, but the Skills Development Management Committee has not been operational since.

[10] Article 10 of Decree No. 9.727-2019

[11] Decree No. 9.727-2019

References

Camões, M. and I. Balué (2015), "Análise de processos seletivos para cargos comissionados no âmbito da administração pública federal", VIII Congresso CONSAD de Administração Pública.

Camões, M. and P. Meneses (2016), Gestão de Pessoas no Governo Federal: Análise da Implementação da Política Nacional de Desenvolvimento de Pessoal, Cadernos ENAP, No. 45, National School of Public Administration, Brasília.

Civil Service HR Division (2017), "People Strategy for the Civil Service 2017-2020", https://hr.per.gov.ie/wp-content/uploads/People-Strategy-for-the-Civil-Service-2017-2020.pdf.

ENAP (2018), Informe de Pessoal: Março 2018, National School of Public Administration, Brasilia.

ENAP/IPEA (2017), Inovação no Setor Público: Teoria, Tendências e Casos no Brasil, Pedro Cavalcante et al. (orgs.), National School of Public Administration, Brasilia.

Institute on Governance (2018), Digital Executive Leadership Program, https://iog.ca/leadership-learning/executive-leadership/executive-leadership-program-digital (accessed 1 March 2019).

OECD (2018a), Embracing Innovation in Government: Global Trends 2018, OECD, Paris, https://www.oecd.org/gov/innovative-government/embracing-innovation-in-government-2018.pdf.

OECD (2018), "Survey on Innovation Skills: Organisational Readiness Assessment" (Habilidades de Inovação: Avaliação de Prontidão Organizacional), unpublished.

OECD (2017a), Innovation Skills in the Public Sector: Building Capabilities in Chile, OECD Public Governance Reviews, OECD Publishing, Paris, http://dx.doi.org/10.1787/9789264273283-en.

OECD (2017b), Skills for a High Performing Civil Service, OECD Public Governance Reviews, OECD Publishing, Paris, http://dx.doi.org/10.1787/9789264280724-en.

OECD (2016a), Engaging Public Employees for a High-Performing Civil Service, OECD Public Governance Reviews, OECD Publishing, Paris, http://dx.doi.org/10.1787/9789264267190-en.

OECD (2016b), "Strategic Human Resources Management Survey", OECD, Paris.

OECD (2015), The Innovation Imperative in the Public Sector: Setting an Agenda for Action, OECD Publishing, Paris, http://dx.doi.org/10.1787/9789264236561-en.

5. Strengthening demand for a skilled leadership in Brazil's federal administration

This chapter assesses the demand for a senior civil service cadre with the skills needed to innovate. Governments can use the appointment system to send clear signals of skills demand if they search for, and appoint senior civil servants based on an objective assessment of those skills. This suggests value in implementing merit-based selection processes for senior civil service positions. Performance management systems also help to maintain demand after selection, by regularly assessing the leaders' deployment of the demanded skills. This chapter looks at both of these in turn and recommends actions to enhance demand for innovation skills in the senior ranks of Brazil's federal public administration.

Identifying leadership competencies (see Chapter 3) and building their supply (see Chapter 4) are two important steps to enhance leadership in Brazil's federal administration. However, to truly ensure that leaders innovate, supply must be matched by a demand for these skills and competencies. The sporadic approach to the supply of innovative leadership skills in Brazil may partially originate from the lack of system level demands for these skills. Brazil's demand drivers creates few incentives to improve supply-side interventions and make a more sustainable federal leadership system moving forward.

Senior civil service (SCS) systems in OECD countries generally ensure demand for a skilled leadership cadre through three interlinked human resources processes: job profiles, appointment (recruitment and selection) and evaluation. Although these processes are relatively nascent in Brazil, some institutions are using them to better attract and recruit senior civil servants with the right competencies, and motivate them to use those skills (see, for example, Odelius [2010]). Three areas where building the demand for innovation-related skills and behaviours could be considered are:

- Job profiles describe what is expected of a particular position in terms of achievements and the specific skills and competencies needed to be successful. They are a clear statement of the skills needed and link the objectives of a position with those of the organisation. Job profiles help to ensure that the right person is appointed to a position and is held accountable for results. In Brazil, job profiles are rarely used in SCS positions.

- Recruitment, selection and appointment processes ensure a match between individuals appointed to a position and the skills identified in the job profiles for that position. However, in Brazil, SCS appointments tend to be made without the support of transparent merit-based criteria or processes.

- Evaluation systems act as a backstop mechanism for the recruitment process, to ensure that the appointed individual performs to expectation (often defined in the job profile and/or performance agreement) and is held accountable for achieving results and leading effectively. In Brazil, there is a lack of effective accountability systems for results, although there is a high level of individual accountability for spending, overseen by the various audit authorities. This imbalance creates an environment where careful spending is far more important than achieving results, and thereby produces a significant and complex set of disincentives for leaders to support any risk associated with innovation.

The lack of tools for defining job profiles, recruitment and performance evaluation in Brazil's senior civil service are not new. The 2010 OECD Review of Human Resource Management in Brazil highlighted that fragmentation and capacity gaps affected public sector performance and the quality of leadership, while also recognising that basing different HRM activities on a common competency framework would help the federal administration build a skilled workforce for good performance. In parallel, there is a vast literature that identifies many fragilities of the Brazilian system. The following sections aim to consider possible ways that Brazil could address each of the categories above.

Box 5.1. Recommendation of the Council on Public Service Leadership and Capability

The 2019 OECD Recommendation of the Council on Public Service Leadership and Capability includes a very specific focus on building leadership capability; in fact, it is the second principle in the Recommendation. The sub-principles reinforce the need to balance supply with a range of demand drivers which not only emphasise merit-based appointments, but also the environment necessary for senior civil servants to perform effectively vis-à-vis the political leadership.

The Recommendation recommends that adherents build leadership capability in the public service, in particular through:

- Clarifying the expectations incumbent upon senior-level public servants to be politically impartial leaders of public organisations, trusted to deliver on the priorities of the government, and uphold and embody the highest standards of integrity without fear of politically motivated retribution.
- Considering merit-based criteria and transparent procedures in the appointment of senior-level public servants, and holding them accountable for performance.
- Ensuring senior-level public servants have the mandate, competencies and conditions necessary to provide impartial evidence-informed advice and speak truth to power.
- Developing the leadership capabilities of current and potential senior-level public servants.

Source: OECD (2019b), Recommendation of the Council on Public Service Leadership and Capability, https://www.oecd.org/gov/pem/recommendation-on-public-service-leadership-and-capability.htm

Job profiles and recruiting for innovation in the senior civil service

Predetermined appropriate qualification and performance criteria for all positions: In order to have a merit-based system, there needs to be a transparent and logical organisational structure, which clearly identifies positions and describes the role and work to be performed by these positions. Criteria for selection, linked to the specific tasks to be performed, help to guide an objective selection process. Merit systems generally strive for criteria which is specific, objective and measurable. This can be a challenge when it comes to behavioural and/or cognitive competencies, which are harder to assess and rank, but which are increasingly vital as predictors of success, particularly at management and leadership levels (see Box 5.2).

Objective and transparent personnel management processes which assess candidates against the criteria specified in (1) above. This includes recruitment/appointment process, and other processes such as performance assessment, pay and dismissal. In general, the following principles should be applied to all of these processes:

- Transparency: In most merit systems, human resources decisions are taken in the open, to limit preferential treatment to specific people or groups. Decisions are generally documented in such a way that key stakeholders, including other candidates, can follow and understand the objective logic behind the decision.
- Objectivity: Decisions should be taken against predetermined objective criteria and measured using appropriate tools and tests that are accepted as effective and cutting edge by the HR profession.
- Consensus: Decisions should be based on more than one opinion and/or point of view. Multiple people should be involved, and efforts should be taken to strive for a balance of perspectives, particularly on processes which are less standardised and open to subjective interpretation, such as interviews or written (essay) examinations.

Open application processes that give equal opportunity for assessment to all potentially qualified candidates. This is key as it helps to ensure that the best person for the job is able to come forward and be considered for the job regardless of their location, demographic characteristics, social status or political affiliation.

Oversight and recourse mechanisms to ensure a fair and consistent application of the system: As with any rule-based system, institutions and processes need to be in place to ensure consistent and fair application. Most countries address these issues through three interrelated mechanisms. The first is by assigning authority for the oversight and protection of the merit system to an independent body with investigative powers and authority to intervene in HR processes when breaches are deemed to have happened or to be imminent. The second is to have recourse mechanisms available to candidates who feel like they have been treated unfairly. The third is to ensure that all people managers have a clear and consistent understanding of the system and their discretion within it.

Most OECD countries have a specific recruitment process for senior civil servants, which often involves a more centralised recruitment process, monitoring and oversight; the use of special recruitment panels or committees to ensure multiple perspectives and accountability of appointment decisions; and in some cases, the use of assessment centres, which aim to assess management and leadership competence through various psychometric testing and simulation activities. Together, these aim to address many of the required elements of a merit-based recruitment system as described above.

Figure 5.1. Common elements of selection processes for senior managers in OECD countries

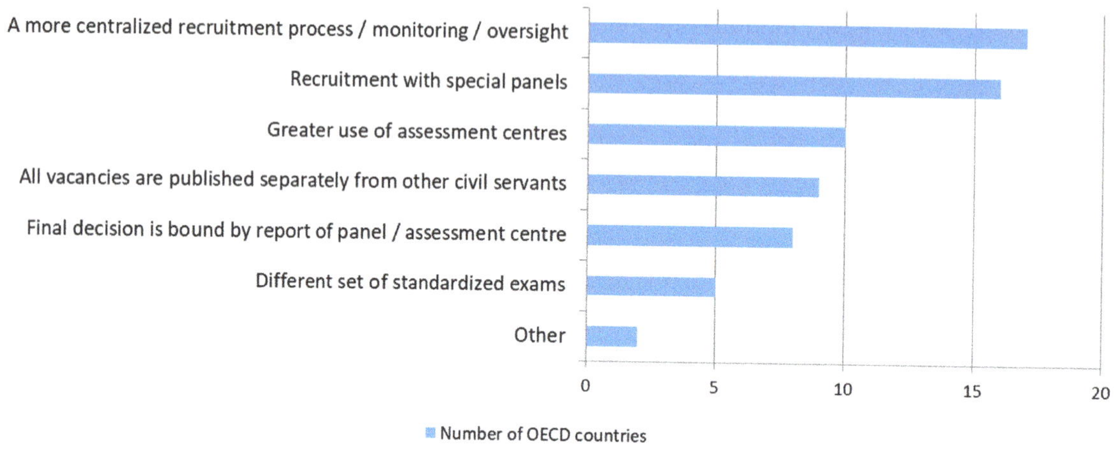

Note: Response of OECD countries to the question Q79a. [If there is a specific selection process for senior manager, does it involve does it involve (select all that are applicable): all vacancies are published separately from other civil servants; a more centralised recruitment process/monitoring/oversight; recruitment is made with special panels; greater use of assessment centres; different set of standardized exams; final decision is bound by report of panel/assessment centre; other
Source: OECD (2016), Strategic Human Resources Management survey"

Box 5.2. Leadership competency assessment

One of the significant challenges when establishing merit-based recruitment for senior leaders is to develop ways to assess the right leadership competencies, which tend to be difficult to evaluate objectively.

Increasingly, OECD countries turn towards specific expertise to support this kind of decision making, often in the form of assessment centres, which use a range of tools such as psychometric tests, simulation exercises and interactive role-play to test candidates' judgement and interpersonal skills in generic situations. The benefit of this kind of input into the decision-making process is that it can be conducted by objective professionals, usually occupational psychologists, who are experts in detecting people's reactions and underlying behavioural competencies. The down side is that it is costly. Therefore, when used, they are usually only used at the end of a process to gain greater insights on the top candidates.

Studies also suggest that the best indicator of a candidate's leadership abilities is their previous demonstrable experience. This can be incorporated into interviews and written exams, then verified through reference checks. For example, if the position requires someone to lead innovation in the delivery of educational services, candidates could be asked to describe a time when they led innovation in a previous job. The key would be to establish a question that is not too specific, and to look for the transferable qualities that demonstrate the leadership competency in question. Multiple assessors should be present, and from different backgrounds, so as to reduce the risk of biasing the process.

As the 2010 OECD report pointed out, the DAS system is generally opaque (OECD, 2010). Understanding the mechanics of political appointments is complex, but is likely to go beyond political party influence and involve different degrees of motivation related to interpersonal relationships and some technical capacity (see, for example, Lopez and Praça [2018]).

Given this complexity in the political system, it is unlikely that Brazil will remove political discretion in appointments, and it would be unwise to do so completely. If selected and managed well, appointees from outside the civil service may bring with them innovative practices and new insights and approaches that can help to improve routines and generate better services for citizens. However, recruiting external expertise does not automatically guarantee an increase in innovation. Unless skills gaps are identified and targeted in recruitment criteria as part of a defined job profile, any increase in innovation capacity due to private sector expertise is by chance rather than by design.

Figure 5.2. Identifying senior managers in OECD countries

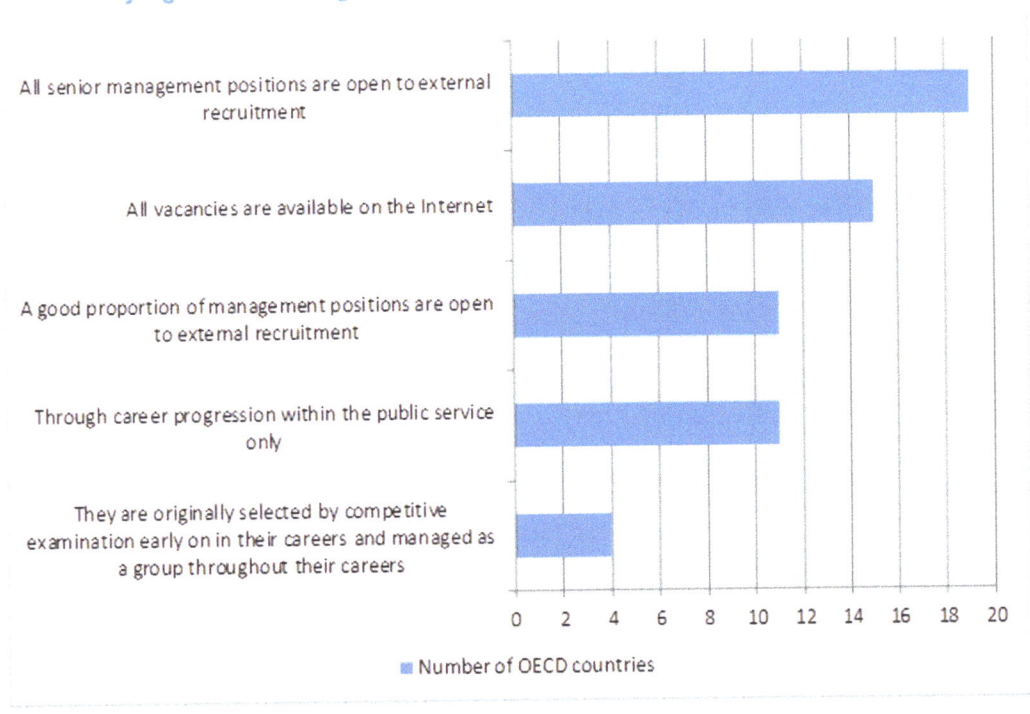

Note: Response to the question: Q76: Irrespective of the existence of an official "senior management", how are senior managers identified? Please check all that apply.
Source: OECD (2016b), "Strategic Human Resources Management Survey".

The same issue arises when appointing from the civil service. Traditionally, "merit" is only a consideration for entrance into the civil service rather than with each position or promotion. The only certainty is that civil servants bring experience and knowledge of the public sector, which is usually lacking in private sector appointees, and can therefore be a necessary and valuable complement (Lopez and Praça, 2018). But without an approach that identifies and uses skills as part of the selection process for senior leaders, skills gaps will continue to exist and could be a strong barrier to transformative, innovative leadership.

By contrast with Brazil, about half of OECD countries have all senior management positions open to external recruitment and vacancies tend to be published on line.

A majority of OECD countries (twenty countries) have one or more processes in place to ensure a degree of merit in political appointments of senior civil servants (Figure 5.3). In 2008, the Australian government introduced a policy implementing transparent and merit-based assessment in the selection of most Australian Public Service (APS) agency heads and other statutory offices working in, or in conjunction with, agencies that operate under the Public Service Act 1999. In Canada, the Clerk of the Privy Council plays a key role in the selection of deputy ministers, based on short lists proposed by the Committee of Senior Officials, and senior personnel administers the process.

Figure 5.3. Accountability for merit in political appointments in OECD countries

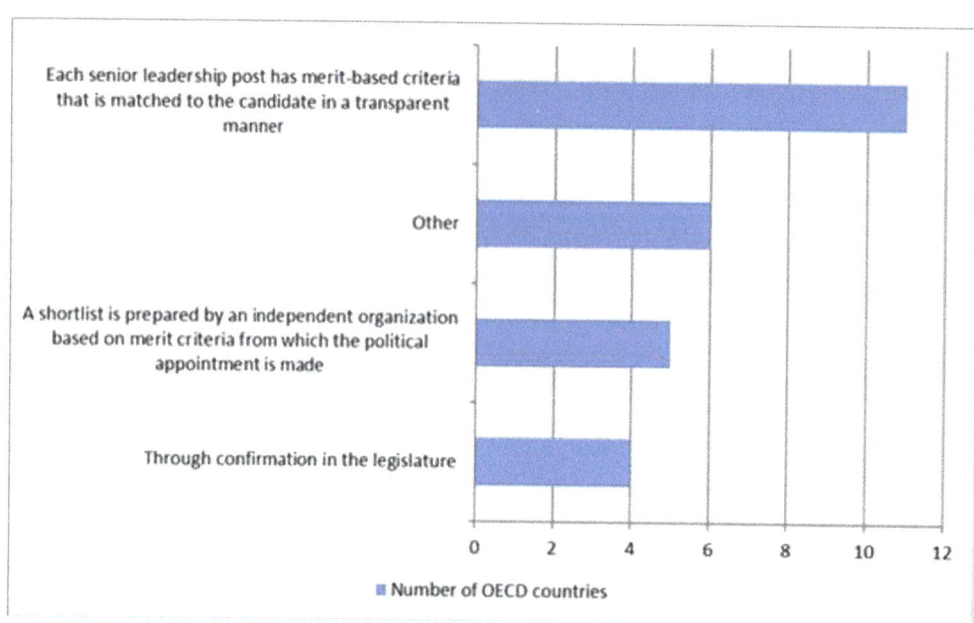

Note: Response to the question: Q95: Are there any processes in place to ensure a degree of merit in political appointments of senior civil servants?
Source: OECD (2016b), "Strategic Human Resources Management Survey".

Regardless of the individual responsible for appointing or the sector from which the appointee comes, there are also systems and mechanisms that can help to ensure each appointee possesses strong leadership skills. For example, the US system enables a thorough vetting of the highest level appointees by the Senate (and the public by extension) and subjects lower level political appointments to the same competency framework (referenced in Chapter 3) as the career Senior Executive Service. While Senate confirmation may not be specifically oriented towards competency assessment, it at least enables a public discussion about whether candidates have the competencies required for the job. The Chilean system uses a transparent meritocratic process to select the top three candidates from which the government may choose (Box 5.3). Meanwhile, Korea's senior civil servants all undertake an initial competency assessment process to enter a pool, from which the government may choose to fill specific positions. In all these cases, the government is free to make the final selection, but there is a system in place to ensure that the government is accountable for its choice.

Box 5.3. Merit-based senior civil service recruitment in Chile and Peru

Chile

Chile's Senior Civil Service System (Sistema de Alta Dirección Pública, SADP) is the region's most established merit-based selection and management system for senior public leaders, which has helped to ensure highly qualified executives are selected to lead the modernisation of Chile's public sector and overall economic and social development. The existence of a centralised, merit-based programme for selecting and managing senior executives places Chile among a growing group of OECD countries that increasingly recognise the value of ensuring merit at the highest levels.

The existence of criteria such as "innovation" and "flexibility" in the competency framework for the SADP provides an opportunity to discuss and further refine this competency, towards more clearly defining what this means in practice.

Peru

The implementation of the 2013 civil service in Peru was fundamentally a large-scale public sector innovation process, as Peru pursued innovations in its civil service structure, as well as the tools and mechanisms that will be used to manage its civil servants. Peru's central human resources management authority, the National Civil Service Authority (SERVIR, in its Spanish acronym) has begun by incorporating some of the principles of public sector innovation and innovation labs in developing policy and tools. For instance, the consultation mechanisms and design processes included early consultation with key strategic partners such as the Ministry of Economy and Finance and the Public Governance Secretariat of the Presidency of the Council of Minister, as well as an opportunity for public comment through their website.

The success of Peru's Public Managers Corp, created in 2008 as a first step to professionalise the management level of Peru's civil service, inspired the new Civil Service Law to further improve the recruitment of the top three layers of all public organisations. The law imposes strict and rigorous selection processes, including evaluation of experience and education, psychological and competency-based assessments, knowledge testing, and a final interview. Once successful, managers are appointed to a position for three years, with the possibility of renewal twice for a total of nine years.

1.   Sources: OECD (2017b), Innovation Skills in the Public Sector: Building Capabilities in Chile, http://dx.doi.org/10.1787/9789264273283-en; OECD (2016a), OECD Public Governance Reviews: Peru: Integrated Governance for Inclusive Growth, http://dx.doi.org/10.1787/9789264265172-en.

Investing in the selection of talented leaders

In Brazil, there are some elements of a selection system for leaders emerging at all levels of government. At state level, experiences from the Public Ministry of Rio Grande do Norte, and the states of Goiás and São Paulo have included some assessment of technical skills and knowledge in selection criteria for appointed positions (Camões and Balué, 2015). Analysis of these experiences suggests that meritocratic processes for selecting senior civil servants contribute to a cultural change, much welcome in a context where public managers are required to have more legitimacy in performing their functions (Ávila et al. [2013] cited in Camões and Balué [2015]).

The federal administration also has some experiences using selection processes for leadership positions, such as the selective processes for DAS announced on the Federal Civil Servant Portal (Portal do Servidor do Governo Federal).[1]

While there is no accepted government framework for leadership, competency-based recruitment processes have started to emerge. Some organisations have implemented competency models to shift towards a more competitive and open hiring process. The Treasury Ministry and Brazilian Development Bank are using various forms of competency-based hiring. Many other organisations that the OECD interviewed expressed interest in moving towards this model, but using competency models for appointment and hiring decisions remains subject to the will of political leaders.

Finally, civil society organisations have also started advocating for a more merit-based and transparent leadership recruitment process in some parts of Brazil's public administration. For example, Vetor Brasil is a non-profit organisation whose mission is to prove to public institutions that running open merit-based leadership recruitment processes can lead to better and more efficient public services, and be a win-win for all parties involved. They do this by running recruitment processes for public agencies who request their services so that they experience the results first hand. Thus far, they have only been invited to work at the state and municipal levels.

Creating legal incentives and improving transparency for greater accountability

The creation of the FCPE in 2016 provided a legal basis on which to develop minimum criteria for all DAS and FCPE positions. Recently, the presidential decree establishing minimal criteria for DAS/FCPE levels states that every individual appointed to any of these positions should have a "clean reputation" and a clean criminal record,[2] as well as a professional profile or academic education compatible with the function to which s/he is appointed. Table 5.1 specifies the additional criteria for DAS and FCPE 2-3, DAS and FCPE 4, and DAS 5-6.

Table 5.1. Minimal criteria for specific DAS and FCPE positions

Criteria (it is compulsory to fulfil one of the following:)	DAS and FCPE 2-3	DAS and FCPE 4	DAS 5-6
Professional experience in related fields	2 years	3 years	5 years
Experience in a trust position in any power, including indirect federal administration	1 year	2 years	3 years in DAS 3 or above
Have a specialist, Master or doctorate degree in a related field	✔	✔	✔
Be a public servant OR military	✔	N/A	N/A
Have attended training in a school of government in related field	120 hours	N/A	N/A

Note: DAS: Senior Direction and Counselling Group; FCPE: "commissioned functions". Minimal qualifications. N/A: not applicable.
Source: Decree No. 9.727 of 15 March 2019, Dispõe sobre os critérios, o perfil profissional e os procedimentos gerais a serem observados para a ocupação dos cargos em comissão do Grupo Direção e Assessoramento Superiores - DAS e das Funções Comissionadas do Poder Executivo - FCPE.

The establishment of minimum criteria is a positive sign and signals a recognition that some level of merit should be considered in the appointment of senior civil servants. However, potential appointees only need to fulfil one criterion among the few indicated in the decree. In addition, selection processes remain optional. Whenever selection processes are organised, the hiring authority still has the discretion to appoint the candidate it wants. Finally, hiring authorities may still appoint individuals that do not fulfil any of the specific criteria listed in Table 5.21. To do so, the ministry above the hiring authority needs to justify why it is appointing someone who does not respect the decree, considering any specificities of the position or the limited number of applicants.

The need to justify the exceptions to the decree creates a degree of public accountability for appointments. This could also help to create data and a public record on such matters for the first time and disseminate information about political appointments. Increasing transparency in the appointment procedures of senior civil servants is particularly useful within systems that appear complex to reform like Brazil's. OECD countries and beyond are also using transparency as a means to increase accountability for decisions that affect values and ethics of the public sector. In Paraguay, for example, public disclosure of civil servants' requests to receive multiple pay is being used by the Secretaria de la Función Pública to try to prevent civil servants from requesting exceptions to the rule of single pay (OECD, 2018).

Transparency needs to be a priority to be effective. This implies an effort to improve active and passive transparency. While many efforts have been concentrated on active transparency (namely open online information), Brazil still needs to improve responsiveness to requests for information. In Brazil, access to public information remains difficult despite the approval of the Access to Information Law in 2012 (Michener, Contreras and Niskier, 2018), with more than half of the requests for information remaining unanswered. Many OECD countries are also using data transparency to improve HR policies. Canada opens by default its datasets related to staffing to facilitate performance monitoring of the staffing system in terms of effectiveness, efficiency and fairness (Government of Canada, 2017).

While still far away from ensuring the kinds of competencies identified in Chapter 3, this new decree may provide a foundation upon which a more thorough skills-oriented system can be developed in the future. The decree can also be useful in the sense that it creates space for the diversity within Brazil's federal administration, where there are many differences among institutions, careers, structures and topics. In this context, the capacity and political will of hiring authorities should influence the success of any transformation of the SCS system.

Aligning incentives to build demand for innovation leadership

Most OECD countries' SCS systems include a specific performance management process, which assesses leaders' job performance against agreed-upon objectives and competencies with their superior(s). Twenty-two OECD countries have specific performance management regimes for the SCS, and in seven OECD countries, senior civil servants have the same performance management regime as other civil servants (OECD, 2019a). Performance management regimes for senior civil servants tend to include performance-based pay (nineteen countries), dismissal as a result for poor performance (seventeen countries) and performance agreements with the minister for the higher hierarchical levels (sixteen countries). Performance criteria usually vary between outcome and output indicators, organisational management indicators and, in some countries, 360° appraisal (OECD, 2019a). By contrast, in Brazil, civil servants and managers in particular know little about the content of the position when they are appointed, as the information is simply not available in most cases (see, for example, Instituto República [2018]). This issue goes broader than the SCS system as the Brazilian administration does not have a standard way to identify, classify or describe positions in the federal administration (OECD, 2010).

Appropriately defined and aligned performance objectives are elements that help to drive a culture focused on results, and accountability of senior leaders. It can also be a very useful tool to make room for more innovation, particularly in a highly risk-averse public sector such as Brazil's. While it is generally difficult to assess innovation as a performance objective itself, outcome-oriented performance objectives that address system improvement and societal outcomes can be an important motivator to encourage innovation. Giving a senior leader the explicit objective to be open to find new ways to address issues and achieve better results can be particularly important in Brazil, where incentives are strongly perceived to align against innovation. A common narrative in the public sector links the risks of innovation with personal career risk. Individuals could find themselves in court and held personally accountable for any perceived failures resulting in loss of public funds, including when undertaking necessary innovation-oriented experimentation.

Managers are incentivised to do only what is explicitly written in the law in order to avoid having their actions scrutinised by control bodies. The general perception is that excessive control creates distortions, leading to an environment where there is no benefit to leading innovation nor transformation – only significant risk to one's own career and prosperity (see, for example, Gaetani [2018]). While the Court of Accounts is well advanced in audits, evaluations, supervisory proceedings and co-ordination across the public sector, a recent assessment of the court also highlights that "excessive evaluation processes or indicators can lead to evaluations that managers see as an administrative burden. Research by ENAP also suggests that managers' responsibilities often consist in responding to control and audit requests (ENAP 2018). In turn, this can undermine a results-oriented culture that is conducive to producing reliable, timely and accessible evidence" (OECD, 2017a).

In the absence of outcome-focused accountability (e.g. for achieving improvements in public services), accountability is focused primarily on controlling inputs and guarding against the perception of wasteful spending and/or corruption. While spending accountability is a fundamental necessity of public administration, it creates a significant disincentive to innovation when not balanced by accountability for results.

Recommendations and roadmap

This chapter has focused on the demand-side of the senior civil service system model, and therefore complements the recommendations from Chapter 4. While one set of recommendations does not preclude progress in the other, they should be considered together to maximise value. For instance, most of the recommendations related to supply seek to create an infrastructure that can develop future leaders. But without engaging with the demand-side, the newly formed infrastructure will have a limited effect and be underutilised.

While the supply-side recommendations are focused on expanding the capacity of the Brazilian system to build, develop and support innovative leaders, the demand side is focused on the people management levers that incentivise the need to develop these skills. These levers are effective and proven signals to people within and outside the system that the public sector demands and expects public sector leaders with the competencies necessary to advance innovation in their organisations.

As discussed in this chapter, traditional levers like job profiles, recruitment and selection processes, and evaluation of senior leaders are some of the most effective and proven ways to create strong demand for innovative leaders. Because these are traditional levers, there is a well-tested path forward. As such, an organisation like the Secretariat of Planning and Management could play a critical role in sponsoring and encouraging the testing of these methods as well as scaling them government wide. The National School of Public Administration (Escola nacional de administração pública, ENAP) can support in the piloting and assessment of different approaches.

Blending these steps with some of the innovation competencies creates recommendations and a roadmap to move forward. The recommendations take into account the recent decree as well as realistic and achievable steps in Brazil's context. As with the supply-side recommendations, these are separated into:

- Immediate: Activities that can begin immediately and are logical next steps based on the understanding of the current system.

- Second-stage: Activities that represent the logical follow-up to the short-term recommendations. These activities will require some reassessment based on feedback and outcomes of the implementation of the short-term recommendations.

- Longer term: Activities that require careful planning, greater investment, more time and a strong systemic foundation. These recommendations will need additional evaluation as changes in complex and dynamic systems are difficult to predict over a long time frame.

Table 5.2. Roadmap for demand-side recommendations

	Immediate recommendations	Second-stage recommendations	Longer term recommendations
Develop merit-based hiring practices that assess innovation competencies	Map and analyse existing initiatives in the federal public administration	Pilot various approaches to competency assessment	Scale across the administration and embed in legislation
Include innovation-oriented objectives in job profiles and performance assessments	Develop templates for job profiles of senior civil servants, including leadership competencies	Pilot regular performance assessment processes	Scale across the administration and embed in legislation
	Communication and feedback		

Immediate recommendations

The new decree creates an immediate opportunity to start using competency-based recruitment and hiring. However, any implementation of new and possibly contested methods requires careful assessment and analysis. This suggests an opportunity to further develop **expertise on recruitment and selection** in ENAP or the Ministry of Economy whose role would be to map activities and systematically gather lessons in a way that can lead to ongoing growth and progress.

The first step could be to **map and assess successful merit-based recruitment initiatives that are already underway in the Brazilian public administration**. With a shift of the status quo, there is an opportunity to use the innovative approach of positive deviance. Within any large community (like the public sector), there are people using uncommon, but successful, approaches and strategies that enable them to find effective solutions to a problem. Within the Brazilian context, there are already some leading institutions such as the Treasury and the Bank of Brazil attempting to achieve better hiring for senior civil servants through competency-based methods. By mapping these examples, ENAP and the Ministry of Economy can learn and share what is already working in the Brazilian context. ENAP's 2019 event "Coffee with Selection" (literaral translation of Café com Seleção) explored merit-based recruitment processes for SCS, to increase awareness across the civil service[3]. A short scan, building on the findings from "Coffee with Selection", could reveal the breadth and variety of different practices, their success factors, and hence their viability for replication and scaling. A further study could help to determine their value added, based on, for example, cost-impact analysis.

In parallel to the research phase and in line with on-going work, ENAP and the Ministry of Economy could **develop a template for SCS job profiles**, which should include, at a minimum, a broad description of the scope of responsibility for the position, a number of more specific objectives, and the skills and competencies that are needed to meet them. These could then be developed for a number of positions. This process should be open and collaborative, collecting input from key stakeholders, including implicated senior managers, auditing organisations and the HR community. At a minimum, these profiles should be developed for any position that will be subject to merit-based recruitment pilot projects, and for those who will participate in performance assessment pilots.

Second-stage recommendations

Building on the ground work conducted above, the Ministry of Economy, with support from ENAP, could **develop pilots to test various merit-based recruitment methods for senior civil servants** with organisations whose leaders are keen to participate. These pilots work best when participating organisations are motivated volunteers, since they require good will and an open mind from all involved. Starting with a "coalition of the willing" rather than imposing through legislation can help to develop quick wins and generate positive momentum forward. Organisations should also be chosen which represent variety – e.g. policy ministries and service delivery agencies, big and small, economic vs. social policy, etc.

– in order to ensure that results are robust and reflect more than one specific context. Pilots could also be designed to test more than one methodology, taking an experimental approach.

In parallel, ENAP and the Ministry of Economy could **launch pilots to develop approaches to ongoing performance assessment of senior civil servants** based on the job profiles developed above. International practice suggests that performance assessment for senior leaders should be kept simple and be used as a way to increase accountability for results. The systems work well when both sides see it as legitimate and beneficial. Considerations similar to those above should guide pilot design. It would also be important to ensure that evaluation criteria encourage innovative behaviour, as they can often have the opposite results. Given that there is no certainty initially, these pilots should not be used to evaluate the effectiveness of a leader in a first phase, but to discover if the process produced better results and the efficacy of the new criteria.

As pilots start to deliver results, it would be useful to use those results to **iterate and improve**. Pilots could be used as a learning opportunity to understand what works and test new ways of thinking. If the public sector is to develop a learning culture, these pilots are an opportunity to demonstrate that culture in practise. Pilot participants and the centre of expertise could be prepared to iterate as new information is gained, scale where there is success and diffuse what works. Organisations could be encouraged to tweak job profiles and the recruitment and selection/performance assessment process as more information, data and knowledge are created. It is unlikely that any single pilot or attempt will be perfect, and therefore, the need for flexibility and adaptability is key. Strong communications and signals from the Ministry of Economy could parlay early success into finding other forward leaning leaders willing to go through the same process.

It could also be useful to **integrate the competency model** (recommended in Chapter 4) into the pilot phases once ready. While this would ideally happen at the outset, pilots do not require a common competency framework to already develop insights into process and assessment. The competency model could be easily integrated into later iterations of the pilots once organisations become comfortable managing the processes involved.

The centre of expertise could also **develop a database** on recruitment and appointments at senior levels. As the minimum qualifications are required for DAS and FCPE due to the 2019 decree, a database could be used to track competencies, job profiles and appointments across the administration, whether merit-based or traditional. This information could better inform further adjustments to the decree, especially looking at impact and patterns on how the decree is being used.

It could be useful to **develop indicators to assess progress and success**. While much of the focus for competency-based hiring is on top-level leaders, one important indicator that could be tracked is how the competency model trickles down into the system. Is the meritocracy within the civil service starting to use these new competencies as well? Collecting and analysing this information gives another indicator if demanding new competencies from top leaders influence the competencies demanded at lower levels of the public sector.

Longer term recommendations

Building on the success of the pilots, the Ministry of Economy could **scale and formalise effective practices** in job profiles, recruitment, assessment and evaluation. This could be accomplished by updating the decree or developing more detailed legislation to provide greater specificity on leadership competencies and evaluation processes.

However, to truly understand if Brazil's leaders are more actively driving public sector innovation, the centre of expertise could **conduct evidence-based evaluations**. Early evaluations should be conducted for each of the pilots to determine whether the innovation competencies and behaviours are being properly utilised. This could include the use of employee engagement surveys. Later, evaluations would have to be expanded to look not only at a change in behaviours, but having a results-driven orientation and more public sector innovation.

As societal and public sector challenges become more complex and more interconnected, innovative leaders do not just represent competencies, but a new approach to solving problems. These challenges are cross-cutting and unable to be solved by one ministry or a single individual. Instead, evaluation could be used to reinforce cross-cutting societal goals that are the priorities for the government. This would encourage collaboration, define priorities and help to support leaders to tackle these complex challenges.

Notes

[1] See, for example: https://www.servidor.gov.br/assuntos/oportunidades/oportunidades-de-cessao (accessed 5 February 2019).

[2] According to Complementary Law No. 64 of 18 May 1990.

[3] For more information, please see https://repositorio.enap.gov.br/handle/1/4098

References

Camões, M. and I. Balué (2015), "Análise de processos seletivos para cargos comissionados no âmbito da administração pública federal", VIII Congresso CONSAD de Administração Pública.

ENAP (2018), "Capacidades estatais para produção de políticas públicas: resultados do survey sobre serviço civil no Brasil", in Cadernos Enap, n°56, https://repositorio.enap.gov.br/handle/1/3233

Gaetani, F. (2018), "A governabilidade da administração em jogo", in: Valor Econômico, 20 April, www.valor.com.br/opiniao/5468781/governabilidade-da-administracao-em-jogo (accessed 17 June 2018).

Government of Canada (n.d.), "Open Government Implementation Plan: Public Service Commission of Canada", http://open.canada.ca/data/en/dataset/43616ec1-2b46-4e74-a0b0-bc3b50229b6e (accessed 24 November 2017).

Instituto República (2018), "Relatório da 3ª Conferencia Anual do Instituto República '"Serviço Público: Desafios no Brasil"', unpublished.

Lopez, F. and S. Praça (2018), "Cargos de confiança e políticas públicas no executivo federal", in: Pires, R., G. Lotta and V. Elias de Oliveira, Burocracia e Políticas Públicas no Brasil: Interseções Analíticas, Institute for Applied Economic Research and National School of Public Administration, Brasilia.

Michener, G., E. Contreras and I. Niskier (2018), "From opacity to transparency? Evaluating access to information in Brazil five years later", Revista de Administração Pública, Vol. 52/4, http://dx.doi.org/10.1590/0034-761220170289.

Odelius, C.C. (2010), "Gestão de desempenho profissional: Conhecimento acumulado, características desejadas ao sistema e desafios a superar", in: Pantoja, M.J., M.R. de Souza Camões and S. Trescastro Bergue (orgs.), Gestão de Pessoas: Bases Teóricas e Experiências no Setor Público, National School of Public Administration, Brasília.

OECD (2019a), Government at a Glance 2019, OECD Publishing, Paris.

OECD (2019b), Recommendation of the Council on Public Service Leadership and Capability, OECD, Paris, https://www.oecd.org/gov/pem/recommendation-on-public-service-leadership-and-capability.htm.

OECD (2018c), OECD Public Governance Reviews: Paraguay: Pursuing National Development through Integrated Public Governance, OECD Publishing, Paris, http://dx.doi.org/10.1787/9789264301856-en.

OECD (2017a), Brazil's Federal Court of Accounts: Insight and Foresight for Better Governance, OECD Public Governance Reviews, OECD Publishing, Paris, http://dx.doi.org/10.1787/9789264279247-en.

OECD (2017b), Innovation Skills in the Public Sector: Building Capabilities in Chile, OECD Public Governance Reviews, OECD Publishing, Paris, http://dx.doi.org/10.1787/9789264273283-en.

OECD (2016a), OECD Public Governance Reviews: Peru: Integrated Governance for Inclusive Growth, OECD Publishing, Paris, http://dx.doi.org/10.1787/9789264265172-en.

OECD (2016b), "Strategic Human Resources Management Survey", OECD, Paris.

OECD (2010), OECD Reviews of Human Resource Management in Government: Brazil 2010: Federal Government, OECD Reviews of Human Resource Management in Government, OECD Publishing, Paris, https://doi.org/10.1787/9789264082229-en.

ORGANISATION FOR ECONOMIC CO-OPERATION AND DEVELOPMENT

The OECD is a unique forum where governments work together to address the economic, social and environmental challenges of globalisation. The OECD is also at the forefront of efforts to understand and to help governments respond to new developments and concerns, such as corporate governance, the information economy and the challenges of an ageing population. The Organisation provides a setting where governments can compare policy experiences, seek answers to common problems, identify good practice and work to co-ordinate domestic and international policies.

The OECD member countries are: Australia, Austria, Belgium, Canada, Chile, the Czech Republic, Denmark, Estonia, Finland, France, Germany, Greece, Hungary, Iceland, Ireland, Israel, Italy, Japan, Korea, Latvia, Lithuania, Luxembourg, Mexico, the Netherlands, New Zealand, Norway, Poland, Portugal, the Slovak Republic, Slovenia, Spain, Sweden, Switzerland, Turkey, the United Kingdom and the United States. The European Union takes part in the work of the OECD.

OECD Publishing disseminates widely the results of the Organisation's statistics gathering and research on economic, social and environmental issues, as well as the conventions, guidelines and standards agreed by its members.

OECD PUBLISHING, 2, rue André-Pascal, 75775 PARIS CEDEX 16
ISBN 978-92-64-48961-5 – 2019

Lightning Source UK Ltd.
Milton Keynes UK
UKHW051919211119
353985UK00001B/8/P

9 789264 489615